WINNIPEG

D0624380

creature ca

Make Your Own • 18 Softies to Draw, Sew & Stuff

Wendi Gratz with Jo Gratz

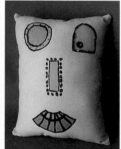

FunStitch
STUDIO
an imprint of C&T Publishing

Text copyright © 2013 by Wendi Gratz

Photography and Artwork copyright © 2013 by C&T Publishing, Inc.

Publisher: Amy Marson

Creative Director: Gailen Runge

Art Director / Cover Designer: Kristy Zacharias

Editor: S. Michele Fry

Technical Editors: Sadhana Wray and Gailen Runge

Cover/Book Designer: April Mostek

Production Coordinators: Jessica Jenkins and Zinnia Heinzmann

Production Editor: Joanna Burgarino

Illustrator: Jessica Jenkins

Photo Assistant: Mary Peyton Peppo

Subject Photography by Diane Pedersen of C&T Publishing, Inc., unless otherwise noted; Style Photography by Wes Stitt; How-to Photography by Wendi Gratz

Published by FunStitch, an imprint of C&T Publishing, Inc., P.O. Box 1456, Lafayette, CA 94549

All rights reserved. No part of this work covered by the copyright hereon may be used in any form or reproduced by any means—graphic, electronic, or mechanical, including photocopying, recording, taping, or information storage and retrieval systems—without written permission from the publisher. The copyrights on individual artworks are retained by the artists as noted in *Creature Camp*. These designs may be used to make items only for personal use. Donations to nonprofit groups, items for sale, or items for display only at events require the following credit on a conspicuous label: Designs copyright © 2013 by Wendi Gratz from the book *Creature Camp* from C&T Publishing, Inc. Permission for all other purposes must be requested in writing from C&T Publishing, Inc.

Attention Copy Shops: Please note the following exception—publisher and author give permission to photocopy pages 19, 27, 38, 48, 49, 54, 58, 62, 67, 68, 75, 76, 83, 84, 92, 98, 104, 107, 117, 118, 125, 126, 133, 134, 140, 148–150, 157, and 158 for personal use only.

Attention Teachers: C&T Publishing, Inc., encourages you to use this book as a text for teaching. Contact us at 800-284-1114 or www.ctpub.com for lesson plans and information about the C&T Creative Troupe.

We take great care to ensure that the information included in our products is accurate and presented in good faith, but no warranty is provided nor are results guaranteed. Having no control over the choices of materials or procedures used, neither the author nor C&T Publishing, Inc., shall have any liability to any person or entity with respect to any loss or damage caused directly or indirectly by the information contained in this book. For your convenience, we post an up-to-date listing of corrections on our website (www.ctpub.com). If a correction is not already noted, please contact our customer service department at ctinfo@ctpub.com or at P.O. Box 1456, Lafayette, CA 94549.

Trademark (™) and registered trademark (®) names are used throughout this book. Rather than use the symbols with every occurrence of a trademark or registered trademark name, we are using the names only in the editorial fashion and to the benefit of the owner, with no intention of infringement.

Library of Congress Cataloging-in-Publication Data

Gratz, Wendi.

Creature camp : 18 softies to draw, sew & stuff / Wendi Gratz with Jo Gratz.

pages cm

ISBN 978-1-60705-784-0 (soft cover)

1. Soft toy making--Juvenile literature. 2. Stuffed animals (Toys)--Juvenile literature. 3. Sewing--Juvenile literature. 4. Handicraft--Juvenile literature. I. Gratz, Jo, 2002- II. Title.

TT174.3.G695 2013

745.592'4--dc23

2013011480

Printed in China

10 9 8 7 6 5 4 3 2 1

contents

DEDICATION
For Jo

ACKNOWLEDGMENTS

Many thanks to all the kids I've sewn with over the years—especially the kids who sewed projects for this book! Alicia, Ben, Caeley, Evelyn, Haley, Hana, Ivy, Izzy, Josie, Liam, Lillian, SeAnna, Sharon, and Sophia, you all were so much fun to work with! An extra-special thanks goes to my daughter, Jo, who made every single project in the book (sometimes more than once). She helped me get everything just right. Jo, you're the best daughter ever. :-)

about this book

Are you ready to learn to sew softies? I hope you'll jump in and have fun! I've arranged the book so you can do it even if you've never used a sewing machine or threaded a needle before. Just start at the beginning, where you'll learn the basics of how to sew a straight line, turn corners, and stuff your softie. Keep going chapter by chapter through all the projects in the book. Each project builds on skills you learned in previous chapters. By the end of the book, you'll sew like a pro and even design your own patterns.

Along the way, I make suggestions for how you can alter patterns to make them your own. You can also go back and revise projects that you did earlier in the book but apply your new skills. Don't let my ideas stop you from trying your own! Sewing softies is fun, and I want you to play! Mix and match fabrics; redraw faces; and, after you get more experienced, even change the shape of some of the pattern pieces. The worst thing that can happen is that you'll make something that looks weird and you won't like it. So start over! No big deal! I've done it many times myself. But sometimes I end up with something that's weird in an awesomely unexpected way, and I like it! You'll never know until you try. So try!

Now—have fun!

1.
getting
started

Words to Know

EMBROIDER: To create designs using thread and special stitches. There are needles and threads designed especially for embroidery.

IRONING: To move an iron back and forth over fabric. You iron to get the wrinkles out of your clothes or to get fabric ready for cutting. However, mostly I'll be asking you to press something, rather than iron it.

PRESSING: To press an iron down on the fabric and then lift it without sliding the iron back and forth. A small craft iron can be handy for reaching small areas.

RIGHT SIDE: The design side of the fabric or the front of the fabric. Sometimes a fabric will have no distinct right or wrong side, so the project maker gets to decide. But pay attention, because you don't want to sew two left feet—or maybe you do!

SEAM: The line of stitching that joins two pieces of fabric.

SEAM ALLOWANCE: The fabric *between* the line of stitching and the fabric edge. The seam allowance is ¼" or ½" for patterns in this book.

WOVEN FABRIC: Fabric made from lengthwise threads linked with crosswise threads. It's not stretchy, which makes it easier for beginners to work with.

KNIT FABRIC: Fabric created using rows of loops (just like knitting by hand, but tiny). It stretches like crazy.

pattern pieces

fabric

Woven fabrics
are very easy
for beginners
to work with.

I recommend gluing all your patterns to cardboard. The cardboard used for cereal boxes is just right. Cardboard is super easy to trace around and stands up better to repeated use. I hope you'll want to make several versions of some of these creatures! Trace or photocopy the patterns from the book, glue them to the cardboard with a gluestick, and then cut them out. Keep pattern pieces tucked into labeled envelopes (one for each project) to keep them from getting lost—especially the small ones.

To use the pattern piece templates, I like to trace around them with a fabric marker or pencil. Then I remove the template and cut out the pattern along the lines. It's much easier than trying to cut the fabric while holding the pattern piece in place.

When you're shopping for fabric, look for woven or quilting cotton. Woven fabric is not stretchy. That's important! There are tons of colors and patterns to choose from. Woven fabrics are very easy for beginners to work with. As you get more experienced, you can use fancy fabrics, such as fleece and fur. I'll introduce them in later chapters.

Always iron your fabric before you try to cut it. It's hard to accurately cut and sew wrinkly fabric. Dial the iron's heat setting to cotton, and use steam.

Many projects in the book call for ¼ yard of fabric. If you go to the fabric store and buy ¼ yard of fabric, they'll cut 9" off a bolt. So you'll have fabric that is 9" long and about 40" wide, which is fine. But if you shop online or at a quilt shop, you'll see lots and lots of fat quarters already cut for you. These are also ¼ yard, but with different dimensions. A fat quarter is made from a half yard of fabric, cut in half again the short way. You get an almost-square piece of fabric, roughly 18" × 20". The proportions are often easier to work with, so choose this option whenever you can.

tools

Here are the tools you'll need for almost every project in the book. Most of these tools are available at craft or sewing stores.

SEWING MACHINE

You can sew any of these projects entirely by hand, but most kids would rather use a sewing machine. If you don't already have a sewing machine at home, here's what to look for when you're out shopping:

- **Get a real sewing machine—not a toy.** You can find them at fabric stores, some department stores, and, of course, sewing machine stores. Many people sell their used sewing machines online. You will *not* find a good machine at a toy store.

- **Get a basic machine.** You don't need fancy stitches. You'll need to sew forward and backward with a basic straight stitch. The ability to do a zigzag stitch will be nice for other projects, but you won't need it for anything in this book. Something with a zipper foot is nice but not needed.

- **Get a machine that's easy to thread.** Any good store will let you try out a machine so you can see how it works. Keep in mind that if you've never threaded a sewing machine before, it will seem *insanely* complicated at first. Trust me, you'll get the hang of it. Some machines have numbers and arrows printed right on the machine to help you. Also, you'll see two bobbin loading types: drop-in (also called top-load) and front-load bobbins. For beginners, drop-in bobbins are easier to work with than bobbins that have a separate bobbin case that is loaded from the front.

Why Sewing Machines Need Bobbins

Of course, you don't need to know exactly how a sewing machine works, but it helps to know the basics.

One big difference between sewing by hand and sewing by machine is that machines need two threads. When you sew by hand, the needle guides the thread from one side of the fabric to the other. In a sewing machine, there are two threads. The top thread goes through the needle and is looped with the bottom thread. The bottom thread comes from the *bobbin*, the small spool that goes in the area under the needle plate.

So every time the machine needle goes down and comes up, a *lock stitch* is created using the bobbin thread. In fact, if you use different color threads for the top and bottom, or if you look between the fabric layers (gently!), you can see the loops.

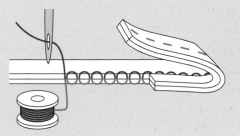

- **Get a machine with a manual.** This is especially important if you're buying a used machine. Machines vary in how they're threaded, how the stitch length is adjusted, and other details. That's why this book comes in handy. Sometimes I'll tell you to look something up in your manual.

- **Finally, try it out to see if you like the feel of it.** The person in the store should be able to help you by letting you test sew.

The person in the store should be able to help you by letting you test sew.

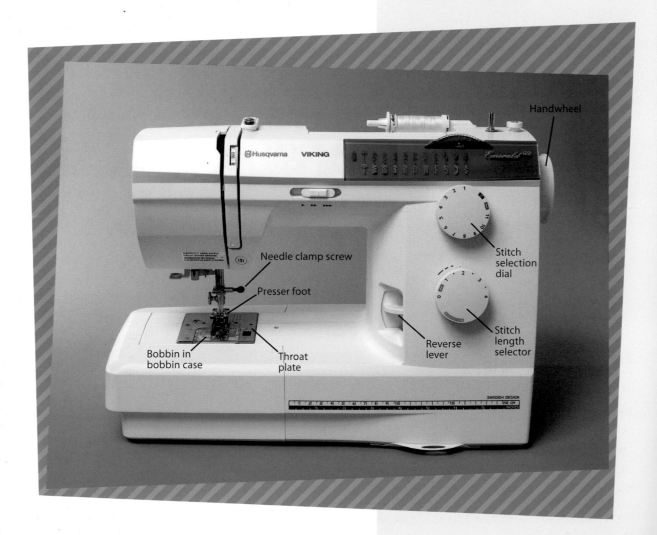

Handwheel

Stitch selection dial

Needle clamp screw

Presser foot

Reverse lever

Stitch length selector

Bobbin in bobbin case

Throat plate

IRON AND IRONING BOARD

You'll use these to iron your fabric before you begin a project, to flatten the seam allowance before you stuff your softies, and for a few other techniques. If you don't have an ironing board, use a folded-up towel on a nonwood surface—or use a *very* thick, multi-folded towel. The steam can go right through a thin towel and ruin the wood underneath it.

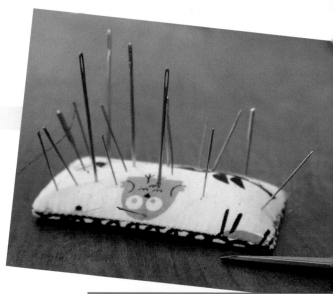

PENS, PENCILS, AND CHALK

You'll need light-colored chalk for marking on dark fabric and darker pens and pencils for marking on light fabric.

If you don't have an ironing board, use a folded-up towel on a nonwood surface—or use a VERY thick, multi-folded towel.

PINS

Get long pins with nice, big, easy-to-see heads.

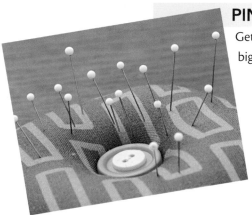

NEEDLE AND THREAD

We'll use the sewing machine for most of the steps in each project, but the last little bit almost always needs to be done by hand. You can use an embroidery needle for sewing up stuffing holes *and* embroidering faces. I like size #5, but you might want to get a pack of assorted sizes and decide what *you* like best.

For sewing, look for all-purpose thread. For embroidery, I like to use DMC six-stranded floss.

SEWING MACHINE NEEDLES

Make sure to always have a few extra sewing machine needles on hand. Look for a pack that says "universal." Needles break, get dull, and need to be changed. Any time my machine acts up, the first thing I do is change to a fresh needle. It's amazing how often that fixes the problem.

Any time my machine acts up, the first thing I do is change to a fresh needle.

SCISSORS

You'll need two pairs of scissors—one for cutting paper and the other only for cutting fabric. Cutting paper will dull your fabric scissors, and then they won't work well for fabric. It's a good idea to tie a ribbon to your paper scissors so you can remember which is which.

SEAM RIPPER

You'll use a seam ripper more than almost any other tool in your kit. It's wickedly sharp, so be careful. The trick to using it properly is to slice just one stitch at a time. Slide the point under a stitch and push the tool forward. The sharp edge at the bottom of the U will slice right through your thread. It seems slow, but that's probably just because you're irritated at having to undo work. :-) It goes pretty fast once you get the hang of it.

I keep a seam ripper at my worktable, another at my sewing machine, and another at my ironing board. That's how often I have to unpick my work. So don't feel bad when it happens to you.

You'll use a seam ripper more than almost any other tool in your kit.

HEM GAUGE

You'll use a hem gauge more often when you start designing your own patterns. That blue arrow slides up and down the ruler part and makes it easy to measure small distances quickly.

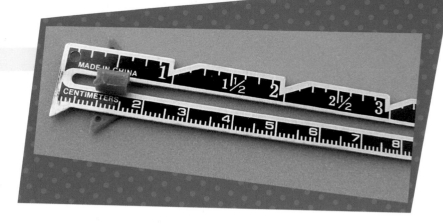

CHOPSTICK

You'll use this tool to help push out the points in your softies. It need not be a chopstick—any long, skinny, not-too-sharp poking tool will work.

TURNING TUBES

These guys are *awesome* for turning tubes of fabric right side out. I'll show you how to use them in Chapter 7 (page 65).

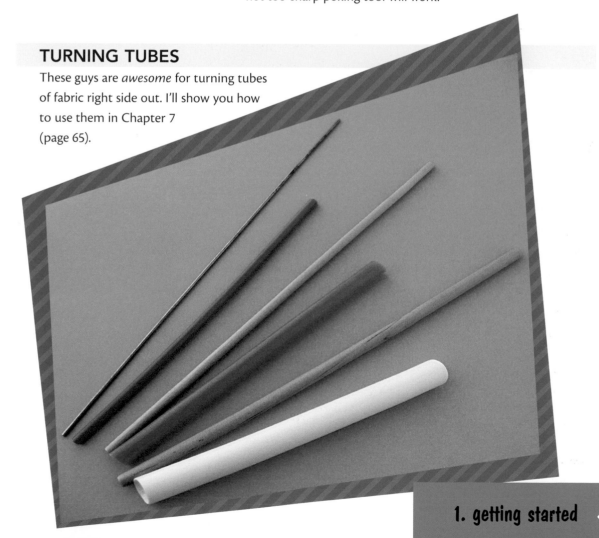

2. basic skills

pinning

Pins are your friends. They're like having lots of extra little hands holding your work together as you sew.

When you pin your layers together, place the head of the pin so it hangs off the edge of your fabric. This way you can pull out the pin when you get to it while sewing. Also, sometimes you'll pin pieces to one layer and then add another layer on top. Pinning in this way keeps your pins from getting lost in the layers.

threading a needle

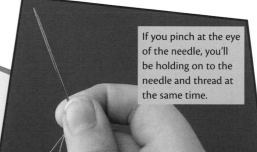

Almost every project in this book uses hand sewing at the end, so you'll have to thread needles. I like to use #5 embroidery needles for sewing. The eyes are a little bigger than a regular sewing needle, making them easier to thread.

How long should you cut your thread? A good measure is the length from your fingertips to your elbow. Make sure you have a clean cut. Raggedy ends are hard to get through the needle.

Poke the end of the thread through the needle. You can wet the end a little if you need to, but it's usually not necessary.

Pull the thread through the needle, leaving a longish thread tail. The other end of the thread (not the tail) is called the working thread.

Working thread ←

Tail →

Knot ←

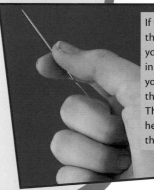

If you pinch at the eye of the needle, you'll be holding on to the needle and thread at the same time.

Wendi says ...

Frustration alert!

Please don't tie the thread to the needle! It makes it almost impossible to fix mistakes! With a thread tail, if you make a mistake, it's easy to slide the needle off the thread, pick out a couple of stitches, rethread your needle, and start sewing again.

When you sew, be sure to hold the needle *at* the eye. That way, you're holding (and pulling) on the needle *and* the thread. You won't pull the needle off the thread by accident. But if you do, no big deal! Thread it again, and you're back on track.

If you don't like holding the eye of the needle, you can hold the needle in the middle and wrap your other fingers around the thread as you pull. That's another way to help keep from pulling the needle off the thread.

how to tie a starting knot

Wendi says ...

If you're left handed and the thread keeps slipping, try switching the needle and thread position to the other hand.

You'll need to know how to tie a starting knot so you can knot the end of your thread after you thread the needle.

Hold the eye of the needle in your right hand, with the point of the needle pointed to your left hand. In your left hand, hold the tip of the thread so it's pointing at the tip of the needle. • • • • • • • • • • • • • ▶

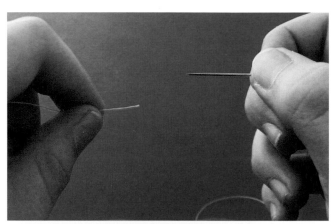

Pass the tip of the thread to your right hand and hold the thread pinched against the needle. With your left hand, wrap the thread four or five times around the needle.

• • • • • • • • • • • • • • • • • ▶

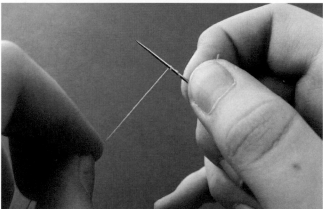

With your left hand, pinch those thread wraps tightly around the needle. Use your right hand to pull the needle and thread all the way through the pinch. When you get to the end of the thread, the wraps magically make a knot! • • • • • • • • ▶

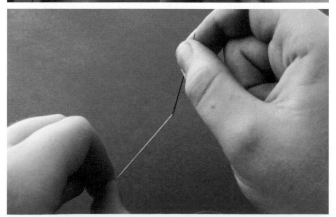

how to tie a finishing knot

Use a finishing knot when you finish sewing.

After you sew your last stitch, take one more little stitch. Don't pull the thread tight; instead, leave a little loop. • • • • • • • • • • • ▶

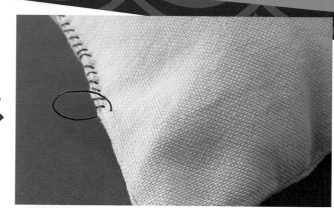

Pass your needle twice through the loop and then pull tight. You just made a knot!

Now, make another knot the same way, just to be safe. • • • • • • • • • • • • • ▶

Stick your needle into your softie right next to your knot. Come up a couple of inches away—it doesn't matter exactly where.

Pull the thread through and snip it off close to the softie. • • • • • • • • ▶

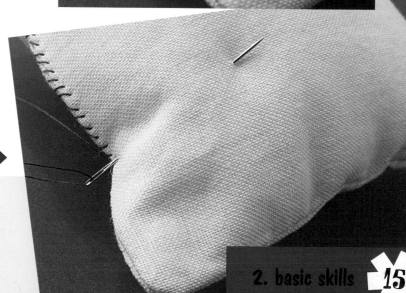

If you massage the softie a bit, that little tail should disappear inside. Neat!

how to tie a square knot

Wendi says ...

If you tie both knots the same way, it's called a granny knot, which doesn't hold nearly as well. Reversing the looping is what makes a square knot hold better.

Use a square knot when you're tying together two tails of thread—like when you sew on a button.

1. Start this knot just like tying your shoelaces. Pay attention—do you loop the right lace over the left lace? Or the left lace over the right lace? I'm a right-over-left person. ● ● ● ●

2. Whatever you did for Step 1, do the opposite for this step. Because I started with right over left, now I do left over right. ● ● ● ●

3. Pull the knot tight. That's a square knot!

4. Snip off the ends, leaving a little tail.

handy measuring tricks

Throughout the book, I'll ask you to estimate certain distances. Sometimes it's a pain to drag out a ruler to measure—especially when you don't have to be that accurate. But your hand can be a good guide. Get out a ruler now and figure out what part of your hand will be your guide for estimating certain lengths.

A ¼″ is the most common seam allowance we'll use, so it's a good idea to know what that looks like. On most kids, it's about the width of your pinkie nail.

We'll also use a ½″ seam allowance on a couple of projects. Try your thumbnail for that measurement.

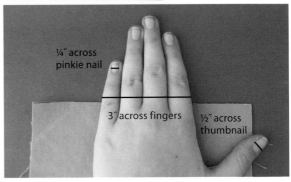

¼″ across pinkie nail

3″ across fingers

½″ across thumbnail

I usually recommend leaving about 3″ for a stuffing opening. You'll estimate this distance for almost every project in the book. The width of all four of your fingers when they're touching is about 3″.

SAFETY

It's mostly common sense.

- **DON'T** stick your finger under the needle on the sewing machine.

- **DO** use a pincushion. If a pin is not in a project, it needs to be in a pincushion—not on a table, *not in your mouth*, not stuck in the arm of the couch. Pins should go straight from the pincushion to your project and then back into a pincushion. No exceptions.

- **DON'T** leave the iron sitting flat on the ironing board. Always stand it up when not in use. Always.

- **DO** be aware that steam can shoot out the sides from under your iron. Don't get your fingers (or body!) too close.

- **DO** remember that if you're sewing your creature for a baby or very young person (under age 3), don't use small parts that they could pull off and swallow. For example, if you want your creature to have eyes, embroider them instead of using buttons, just to be safe!

Pins should go straight from the pincushion to your project and then back into a pincushion. **NO EXCEPTIONS.**

Always stand the iron up when not in use. **ALWAYS.**

3.
straighten up and stuff it

Words to Know

HAND STITCHING: To sew with a needle and thread by hand, instead of with a sewing machine. It is *not* poking yourself with a needle. Nor is it sewing your hands together! :-)

RAW EDGE: The cut edge of fabric that is not stitched or finished.

When it comes down to it, a softie is just a pillow with a fancy shape. It might be a few shapes sewn together with stuff growing out the seams, but at its heart, it's a three-dimensional fabric shape with stuffing. Just like a pillow. We're going to start with a pillow so you can learn the basic skills you'll need for all the softies in this book. You'll learn to sew with the machine, how to stuff, and how to close the stuffing opening by hand stitching.

sewing straight lines

If this is your first time using the sewing machine, you'll want to practice sewing on paper first. It's a good way to get a feel for the machine, and it's easier to work with than fabric.

1. Trace or make a copy of the practice lines and the box on the right. ● ● ● ● ● ●▶

2. Start with the straight lines. Set the stitch length on your sewing machine to 2.5, or about 10 stitches per inch. Lift up the presser foot (using the lever at the back or side of the needle), and put your paper under it so the needle will go right into the line. Lower the presser foot. ● ● ● ●

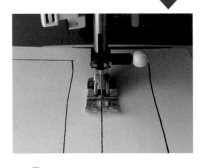

3. Push on the foot pedal to start sewing. See how the machine pulls the paper through the machine for you? All you have to do is steer the paper a little bit—*and your fingers don't need to go anywhere near the needle.* Try to sew right on the line. Experiment with different amounts of pressure on the pedal to see how much you can slow down or speed up. Repeat this step as many times as needed until you feel comfortable steering and controlling the speed.

4. Now we'll get a little bit trickier. Let's practice sewing *to the side of the line.* Repeat Steps 2 and 3, but this time, instead of having the needle go through the line, set things up so that the edge of the presser foot goes beside the line. ● ● ● ●

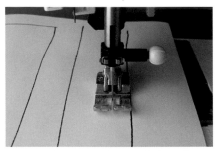

You should end up with a straight line of holes. Are your holes ¼" away from the line? Are they more than ¼" or less?

5. Let's practice a ½" seam allowance. This time forget about the lines you drew on the paper, because your fabric won't have sewing lines printed on it! Instead, you're going to pretend that the paper's edge is the edge of your fabric. You'll sew just like you will on the real thing.

Take a look at the metal plate that the needle goes into. It's called the *throat plate*. There should be lines with measurements engraved into the metal to the right of the needle. ● ● ● ●

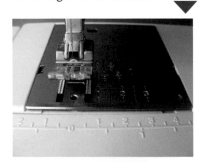

Find the line ½" away from the needle. You may want to mark it with a strip of masking tape to help you keep an eye on the line. Now sew so that the paper's edge runs right along that ½" marking. ● ●

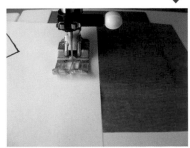

You should have a straight line of holes exactly ½" from the edge of the paper. Keep practicing until you're happy with the results.

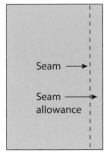

Seam →

Seam → allowance

This practice will help you with the real thing. Soon you'll be sewing straight seams with even seam allowances on fabric.

turning corners

Now that you've mastered sewing a straight line, let's turn some corners. Go back to sewing right on the line and get ready to practice with the box on the practice page (page 19).

1. Sew on the line of one side of the box. Stop when you get near the corner. Use the handwheel (see the sewing machine diagram, page 8) to sew exactly to the corner of the box, and leave the needle down in the paper.

2. Raise the presser foot. Turn the paper carefully until you're lined up to sew the next side of the box. ● ● ● ●

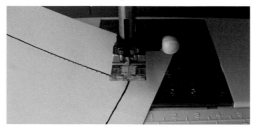

See? You can swivel the paper as much as you want, and the needle holds it in place. You'll start right where you stopped, and you'll get a perfectly sharp corner.

3. Lower the presser foot and sew the next straight segment.

4. Repeat Steps 1–3 until you've worked all the way around the box.

5. Try it again, but this time sew ¼" outside the edge of the box, just as you did in Step 4 of Sewing Straight Lines (page 20). Things get trickier here because you have to guess where your corners will be. Don't worry if you're off the first few times. Soon you'll be a pro at estimating ¼".

6. Finally, try it again using a ½" seam allowance all around the box, just as you did in Step 5 of Sewing Straight Lines (page 20). This time you're going to estimate ½". Practice a couple of times. You'll get the hang of it.

Got it? Yay! That's exactly what you'll do to sew the pillow project. Now throw away that needle. Sewing through paper makes needles dull. If you keep using it, it will mess up your fabric.

How to Change the Sewing Machine Needle

1. Look for the needle clamp screw (see the sewing machine diagram, page 8) to the right of the top of your needle. On newer machines, this screw usually has a fat knob. On older machines, you may have to get a screwdriver from your mom's or dad's toolbox.

2. Hold on to the needle and *loosen* the screw. *Don't unscrew it all the way!* It can be tricky to get it back in, so loosen it just until you can pull the needle out. The needle has a flat side. As you pull the needle out, notice which way the flat side faces. In most machines, it faces away from you, but in some machines, such as Singer Featherweights, it goes to the side. Throw away the old needle.

3. Take a new needle out of the pack. Look at the top of the needle. It should be flat on one side. Hold it so the flat part faces the same way as it came out, or check the manual if you're not sure. Slide it up into the hole. Make sure it goes all the way in!

4. Hold the needle in place as you tighten the screw.

Done!

stuffing your softie

The Number 1 rule of stuffing is *don't be skimpy*! You don't need your pillow or softie to be rock hard, but you definitely want it to be plump and to look full. (I like it to feel about as firm as a marshmallow.) It will take *way more* stuffing than you think. I've been doing this for years, and I'm always astonished at how much stuffing it takes to fill a softie.

1. Take some stuffing out of the bag and pull it apart, making smaller clumps. This will keep your finished project from looking lumpy.

2. Start stuffing into the part farthest from your stuffing opening. If it's a corner, pack smaller clumps of stuffing right into the point. You can use your chopstick to do this. Work your way out with larger clumps as you move into larger areas.

3. Keep working your way toward the stuffing opening. Make sure each area is nicely full and smooth before you move past it. Once you stuff the main body, all that stuffing blocks access to arms, legs, and other bits that stick out. It can be really hard to go back in and add a bit more. For a square pillow, for example, fill each of the four corners and make sure they look good before you start to fill up the big middle part.

4. When you get to the stuffing opening, make sure you fill it right up to the top. Some stuffing should actually peek out of the opening. This will help prevent a dent where you sew the softie up.

sewing up the opening

Most of the sewing in this book will be on the machine, but sometimes you just have to use a needle and thread. This is one of those times. You'll use a whipstitch, because it's the easiest way to sew up a softie or pillow.

1. Before you sew, make sure you press the raw edges under around the stuffing opening. This will give you crisp folds to follow when you sew up the opening. • • • • • • • • • • • • • ▶

2. Thread a needle with thread that matches your softie and tie a knot at the end (page 14). Put the needle in the stuffing opening and pull it out through the creased fold you made in Step 1.

The tail of the thread should be inside the softie. The thread should look like it's growing out through one of the folded edges. • • • • • • ▶

3. Pinch the edges of the opening together so the folds line up. If you turn it sideways, it should look like a little mouth, with the folds being the top and bottom lips. I find it's easiest to sew if I hold the project sideways. You'll soon discover what's most comfortable for you.

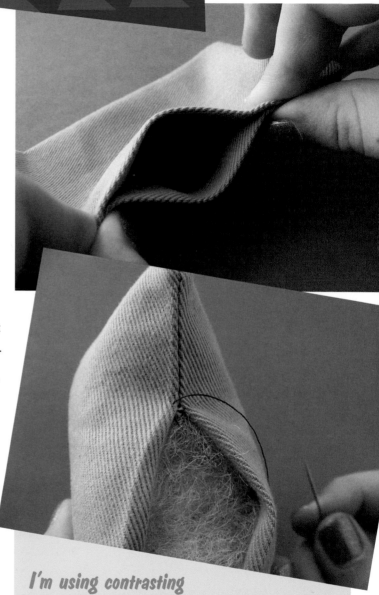

I'm using contrasting thread here so you can see it. You should choose thread that matches your fabric.

3. straighten up and stuff it 23

4. Starting at one edge of the opening, take the first stitch inside the "mouth" to hide the knot, and go through the top "lip." Make the next stitch very close to the first, going up through the bottom lip, then through the top lip. Pull it tight. ● ● ● ● ● ● ● ● ● ● ●▶

5. Again, very close to the previous stitch, poke the needle up through the bottom lip and then through the top lip. Pull it tight.

Make sure you're always stitching in the same direction, up through the bottom lip and then through the top lip.

6. Repeat over and over again until the opening is closed. Make sure you're always stitching in the same direction, up through the bottom lip and then through the top lip. ● ● ● ● ● ● ● ●▶

You should start to see a row of tiny stitches marching across the lips you're stitching closed. Keep the stitches small and very close together for the best results.

7. Tie a knot at the end of your thread (How to Tie a Finishing Knot, page 15). Poke your needle into the softie, very close to your last stitch. Come out anywhere. ● ● ● ● ● ● ● ● ● ●▶

8. Pull the thread tight and snip it off close to the softie. Squeeze the softie and the tip of that tail will disappear, forever hidden in the body. :-)

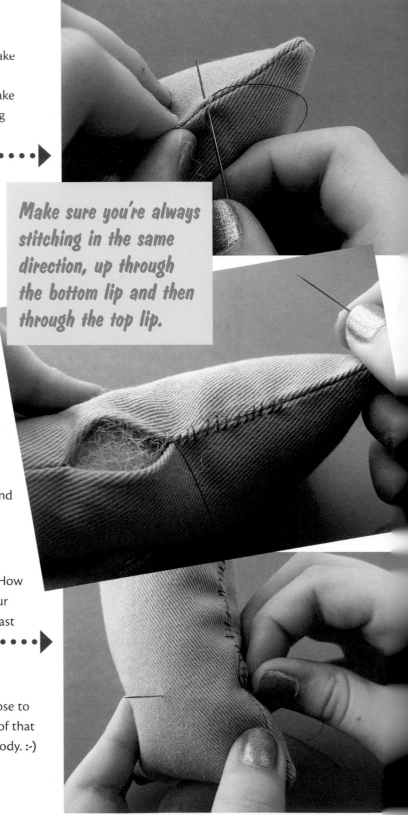

mr. roboto

Finished pillow: 8″ × 10″

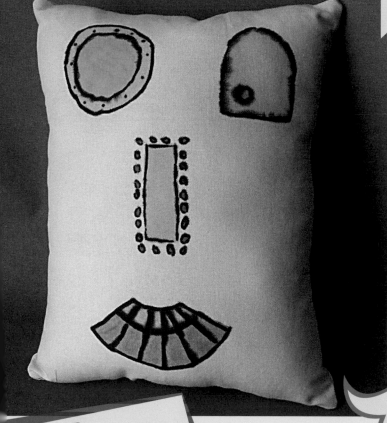

MATERIALS

- ⅓ yard fabric or 1 fat quarter
- Iron-on transfer pen or pencil (I use Sulky iron-on transfer pens.)
- Fabric markers (I use Marvy markers.)
- Freezer paper (available at the grocery store) or Quilter's Freezer Paper, at quilt fabric shops
- Fiberfill stuffing

Make a robot head pillow and practice skills you'll need for making almost all softies.

Mr. Roboto says ...

Keep in mind that your transfer will be the mirror image of what you draw. If you want my face to be exactly the way you drew it, tape the paper face on a window and trace the design onto the back of the paper. Ta-da! Now it will be just like you planned!

make it

DRAW THE FACE

1. Cut 2 rectangles of fabric, each 9″ × 11″.

2. Choose robot parts (page 27) for the eyes, nose, and mouth—or draw your own! Trace the ones you want on a clean sheet of paper using an iron-on transfer pen. If you photo-copy the page, you can trace right over the lines with your transfer pen. ● ● ● ● ● ● ● ●➤

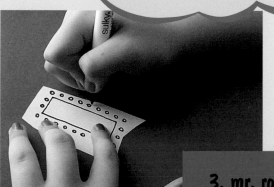

3. Cut out the robot parts. Leave plenty of white paper around the edges, so you have something to hang onto when you iron. Arrange the parts on the front of the fabric, ink side down. Remember that ½" around the edge of the rectangle will be the seam allowance that ends up inside the pillow. Keep your designs toward the center of the rectangle so they don't get lost.

4. Iron over the back of each piece of paper to transfer the image to the fabric. It should only take a few seconds. ● ● ● ●

It doesn't have to be a perfect transfer, because you're going to trace over the lines with a dark marker.

Wendi says ...

Drawing on fabric can be a pain because pencils, crayons, or markers tend to grab the fabric and scrunch it up when you draw. The trick is to make the fabric stable so that it acts more like paper. That's where freezer paper comes in. When you stick it to your fabric, it acts as a stabilizer.

Mr. Roboto says ...

Some fabric markers say you need to heat set them, either with an iron or in the dryer, before washing. If you plan to wash me, check the package instructions to see if you need to set the ink. If so, do that now.

5. Cut a piece of freezer paper slightly bigger than the piece of fabric. Place the fabric face down on the ironing board. Then place the freezer paper shiny side down on the fabric. Turn off the steam on your iron. Iron the freezer paper so it sticks to the back of the fabric. Now you're ready to color!

6. Draw over the transferred lines to outline and color in your robot. ● ● ● ●

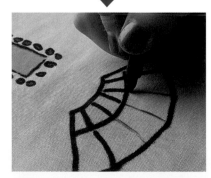

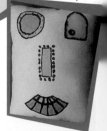

When you're done, simply peel off the freezer paper. It comes off without leaving any sticky stuff behind. Cool!

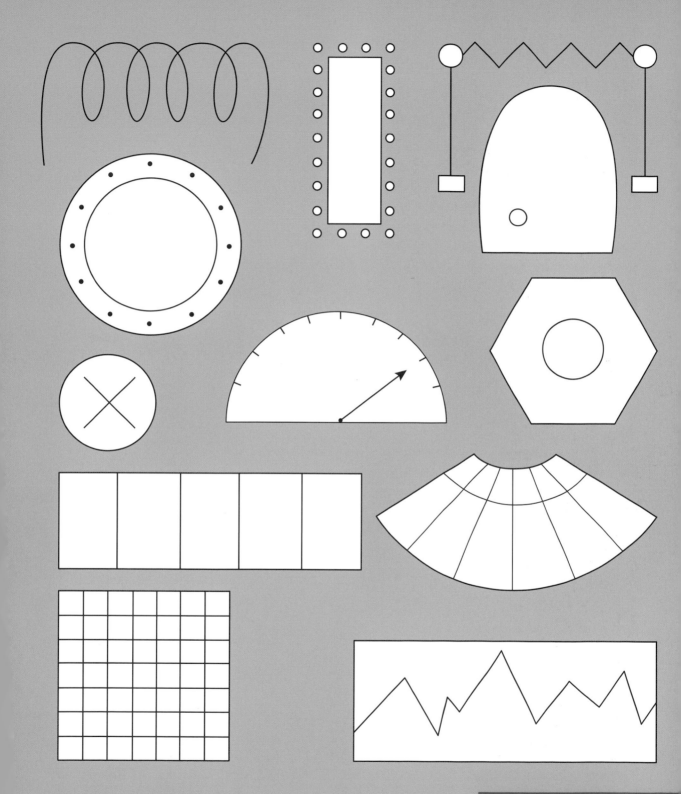

MAKE THE PILLOW

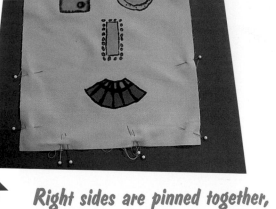

1. Place the plain 9" × 11" piece of fabric face up. Then place the robot head face down. Line them up all around the edges and pin them together (see page 12). Leave an opening 3"–4" wide so you can stuff the pillow after sewing. I mark the beginning and end of the stuffing opening with two pins to remind me where to start and stop when I'm sewing. • • • • • • • • • • • • • • • ▲

Right sides are pinned together, but the color shows through the back, so you can see the face.

2. Using a ½" seam allowance, sew all around the pillow. Backstitch at the beginning and end so your stitches don't pull loose.

3. Turn the pillow right side out. Use a chopstick or something similar to gently poke out the corners.

4. Neatly press the raw edges of the stuffing opening so they line up with the rest of the pillow. • • • ▼

Wendi says ...

Backstitch means "sewing backward." You backstitch for just a few stitches at the beginning and end of your stitching to work like a knot. On most machines, you hold down a button or flip a lever to go backward. It's often marked with something that looks like a U-turn, but it will vary by machine. Check your user manual.

5. Stuff the pillow. Use plenty of stuffing so it's nice and full, with no dips or wrinkles at the edges.

6. Sew up the opening (see page 23).

Done! Toss it on a chair and then make some friends for it.

It's always a good idea to have a couple of spare heads. :-) Can you make some other kinds of heads? How about a cat? A clown? An alien? A dog?

Ben decided to make a round robot head. You can do this too after you learn how to sew curvy lines in Chapter 7 (page 60). I love how he used different colors for the top and bottom of the mouth.

Of course, you can go beyond heads! Write your name in fun bubble letters. Fill the space with a pretty pattern. Draw a big flower—or a field of smaller flowers. What else can you imagine?

4.
the eyes have it

Words to Know

APPLIQUÉ: To sew (or glue) small pieces of fabric onto larger pieces of fabric.

PAPER-BACKED FUSIBLE ADHESIVE: Also called fusible web. Sheets of paper with heat-activated glue that are used to stick fabric to other porous surfaces.

If you're making something with a face, pay special attention to the eyes. They bring the whole face to life! You can even leave the nose and the mouth off completely, but a face without eyes just isn't a face.

Let your imagination go wild with materials to use for eyes—markers, beads, custom shapes cut from the lids of plastic containers. I once had a student who made extra-special eyes with shrink plastic! We're going to cover the most common options here, with tips on making them match (if you want them to) and giving them expression.

stitched eyes

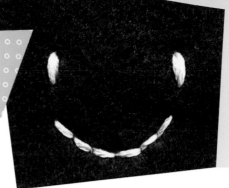

The easiest eyes are simply little stitches. I love the cartoony look of them. They're safe for even the youngest babies. Here's how to make them.

Let your imagination go wild with materials to use for eyes

1. Draw a little up and down line where you want to place the eye. The length depends on the size of your softie, but this method works best for small eyes. Don't make the line any longer than about ¼".

2. Draw a matching eye—as close to the same length as possible—where you want it. After you stitch the eye, it will look bigger. Draw both eyes now so you have matching guides to get the same finished size.

3. Thread your needle with embroidery thread, yarn, or regular sewing thread. Tie a knot at the end, leaving a looooong tail—at least 3" long.

4. Starting at the bottom of the eye, bring your thread up from the back. Go back into the top of the eye and pull your thread through. Not too tight! You don't want to crinkle up the fabric behind your eye. That's one stitch.

5. Take a look. If the eye isn't as full as you want it to be, repeat Step 4 for another stitch. And another. And another. Keep taking stitches until the eye is as fat as you want it to be. I often take 2 or 3 stitches. Keep track of how many stitches you use so you can make the other eye exactly the same way.

6. Remember that long tail you left in Step 3? Now you're going to put it to use. Tie your working thread to your tail in a square knot (page 16) and snip off the ends. Not too close! Leave at least ¼" so your knot doesn't come undone.

7. Repeat Steps 3–6 for the second eye.

No Scarface!

Are you wondering why you don't stitch the first eye, pass the thread across the back, stitch the second eye, and *then* tie your knot? Well, if your fabric is *really* thick *and* a dark color you can do that, but it's risky. Most of the time you stitch the eyes using dark thread, which has a tendency to show through almost *any* fabric when it's stuffed. It's no fun to get through all the work of making a softie and then find out—after you stuff it—that there is a big ugly line showing right through the middle of the face. I say, better safe than sorry. Take the extra minute to tie off the thread behind each eye.

button eyes

These are just as easy as stitched eyes, but they are *not* safe for babies. When deciding what kind of eyes to use, think about who is going to be snuggling your softie.

Attaching buttons is a lot like sewing stitched eyes. The only difference is you will slide the needle and thread through a button in Step 4 (page 31). Easy peasy. Starting off and tying the knot are exactly the same.

The Look

Here are a few things to think about when you use button eyes. Remember, there are no right or wrong answers. You just need to decide what's best for your project.

Do you want to use buttons with two holes or four holes?

I use two holes most often, but four holes are absolutely perfect for zombies. Sew them on with X's, and you have instant zombie eyes.

Do you want to sew on the buttons using thread that matches the button or thread that contrasts with it?

Contrasting thread adds an extra speck of color, which can be great, but sometimes you just want a solid black eye.

If you choose two-hole buttons, which way do you want the eyes turned?

This is especially important if you use contrasting thread. The stitching will make a line on the eyes. Do you want that line to go up and down? Up-and-down often makes the finished face look cheerful and open.

Or do you want the line to go side to side?

This can make the face look sleepy—great for a bedtime toy.

Or do you want it to slant in or out?

Try different sizes and arrangements before you sew them in place. See what you like best!

safety eyes

Safety eyes are specialty eyes that lock in place. No sewing needed! I don't know why they're called safety eyes though, because they're not safe for babies. They should really be called easy eyes! On the back, the eye has a ridged shank—the part you will use to attach the eye to the softie face. There's a special washer that won't come off once you put it on, so make sure it's where you want it before snapping it closed! You can get basic black domes in various sizes at everyday craft stores. Specialty stores and online shops carry safety eyes in all kinds of colors and with pupils shaped to look like the eyes of different animals. Fancy!

Poke a small hole in your softie exactly where you want the eye to go. Use just the tip of very sharp scissors or—very carefully—the point of your seam ripper. Don't make the hole too big! It should be just big enough for the shank of the eye to fit. Slide the shank through the hole. Once you are happy with the placement, push the special washer onto the shank, as far as it will go.

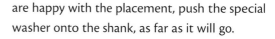

the whites of the eyes

Stitches, buttons, and safety eyes are all good. But what if you want your eyes to be bigger or more expressive? That's where you'll want to add some whites to those eyes. The stitches, buttons, and safety eyes become pupils in larger eyes made of fabric or felt.

You have two basic options here: Sew the white in place while attaching the pupil, or glue it in place.

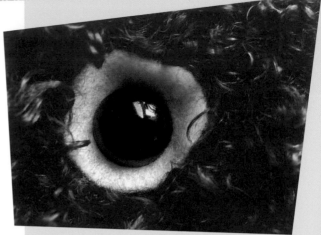

SEWN

The simplest way to add whites to your eyes is to cut a circle of felt bigger than whatever you're using for the pupil. Sew this felt in place when you sew on the pupil. Or slip the shank of a safety eye through a simple white felt circle and then into the fabric of the softie. Do the same with a stitched eye or a button eye, and you have an eye with some white showing. This is especially helpful if you're working with furry fabric, where the eye can get a little lost in the fur.

The simplest way to add whites to your eyes is to cut a circle of felt bigger than whatever you're using for the pupil.

Because the white of the eye is not attached around the edges, but just in the center, the felt eye may want to curl around those edges. That's fine if you don't make it too much bigger than the pupil.

GLUED

If you want really big whites so you can play with the placement of the pupils in the eye, you can use something called paper-backed fusible adhesive. Here's how it works.

1. Draw or trace your eye shape onto the paper side of the fusible adhesive. • • • •

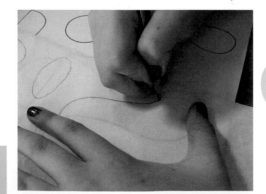

2. Roughly cut out the shape. Don't cut exactly on the lines. Leave a little extra all the way around.

3. Follow the directions of the brand you're using to fuse the bumpy (nonpaper) side of the adhesive to the back of your fabric. Let it cool.

creature camp

4. Cut out your shape along the lines you drew. If your softie will have 2 eyes, prepare 2 pieces of fabric with the paper-backed adhesive. Put them together, with fabric sides touching and paper sides out. Cut along the lines you drew in Step 1. Cut through both layers of fabric at the same time. Now you have 2 eyes that match exactly, mirror images. ● ● ● ▶

5. Peel off the paper backing. The back of the fabric beneath the paper will be shiny and smooth. That's the adhesive.

6. Position the eyes exactly where you want them, with the adhesive down and the fabric up. Follow the fusible brand's instructions to iron them in place. The iron will melt the adhesive, and the fabric eyes will stick to the fabric. Magic!

7. After you fuse the whites in place, let the adhesive cool. Then add the pupils. Here's where you can get really expressive. ● ● ● ●

Bigger pupils tend to look friendlier. Smaller pupils can look mean or scared.

Put the pupils right in the middle of the eyes to make them look scared or surprised.

Put the pupils down low to make the eyes look menacing.

Shift the pupils both to one side to make your eyes look in a particular direction.

Put the pupils in completely different places to make them look wacky.

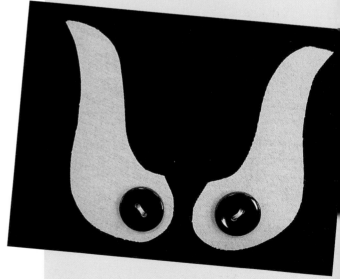

How would striped or spotted fabric look? Play around to see what looks best on *your* softie!

And, of course, whites don't have to be white at all! How about a nice acid green?

the spooky crew

Finished pillow: 18″ × 18″

MATERIALS

- 18″ × 18″ pillow form or loose pillow stuffing

- ⅝ yard dark fabric

- Scraps of fabric for eyes

- Paper-backed fusible adhesive (I use Pellon Heavy Duty Wonder-Under.)

- Assorted black buttons

Make a spooky pillow for your room. You can use as many or as few pairs of eyes as you like. This one is a whole pillow *full* of eyes. Try one with stitched pupils instead of buttons. Or take the eyes pattern to a copy machine, enlarge your favorite shape until it nearly fills the pillow, and use that for your pattern. Or make two pillows—one with the eyes looking left, and the other with the eyes looking right. Arrange them on your bed so the pillows are looking at each other. Have fun with it!

make it

1. Cut 2 squares 19″ × 19″ of dark fabric.

2. Choose which eyes you want to use (patterns on page 38) and how many. Follow the Glued instructions (page 34) to glue the eyes to a square piece of fabric, using fusible adhesive. Remember that ½″ all the way around the 19″ square will be in the seam allowance, so keep your eyes away from that zone.

The Spooky Crew says ...

If you don't want to sew on a bunch of buttons, take a shortcut with fabric markers! Get a nice black marker and draw in the pupils. It's not quite as nice-looking as buttons, but it's fast. :-)

3. It's time to play again. Work with one pair of eyes at a time. Decide what size buttons to use and how they should be positioned in the eyes. Stitch them in place. Repeat until all the eyes have button pupils.

4. Place your finished eye-filled square face up on your workspace. Place the other piece of dark fabric face down on top of the eye-filled square. Line up all the edges. Pin the layers together around 3 sides.

5. Using a ½″ seam allowance, sew the pillow front and back together around 3 sides, if you're going to use a pillow form. If you're going to fill the pillow with loose stuffing, you can sew the fourth side partially closed, still using ½″ seam allowance and leaving a 3″–4″ opening for turning and stuffing. Backstitch at the beginning and end.

6. Turn the pillow right side out. Press the raw edges of the opening nice and flat.

7. Slide in the pillow form or stuff it with loose stuffing.

8. Stitch the opening closed (see page 23).

9. Toss the pillow on your bed and enjoy!

4. the spooky crew

your turn!

Take a look at the spooky crew that Lillian created! She made hers chock-full of eyes in all kinds of crazy colors and patterns. That's a lot of spooky critters hiding in the dark! She also decided to take the fabric marker shortcut.

Now that you know how to stick fabric to fabric, you can make anything you can draw! Maybe add a speech bubble showing what the owner of those spooky eyes is thinking?

You can also combine your skills from Chapter 3 with this one. Make another robot pillow using fusible adhesive and colorful fabric instead of the markers to add color. Have fun!

5.

stitchy situations

You know how to draw on fabric with markers, how to sew on buttons, and how to appliqué with fusible adhesive. (You didn't know you knew that last one, huh? Yep, you can appliqué. You did it in Chapter 4.) Now you'll learn another method for decorating the surface of your fabric—embroidery.

A few basic embroidery stitches are good to know for a few reasons.

- **Sometimes the fabric you want to use is too dark for markers** to show up well. Embroidery works on any fabric, and the thread is available in a wide range of colors—even glow in the dark!

- **Marker lines are flat.** Embroidered lines are raised and bumpy. They can add an interesting texture to the fabric surface.

- **Fabric markers are usually pretty fat.** Embroidery lets you stitch finer lines and details.

- **You can stitch just about any design with four basic stitches.** Grab a needle and thread, hoop up some fabric, and let's learn them.

running stitch

Running stitch is the easiest stitch there is. It gives you a nice dashed line, which makes fun accents and textures.

1. Draw a line on the fabric and put the fabric in a hoop. Thread your needle and tie a knot at the end of the thread.

2. Bring your thread up from the back of your work at the start of the line you want to stitch. • •

3. Push your needle down through the fabric a stitch length away and pull the thread through to the back. That's one stitch. • •

4. Push your needle back up a stitch length away and pull your thread through to the front. • •

5. Push your needle down a stitch length away and pull the thread through to the back. • •

6. Repeat Steps 4 and 5 until you get to the end of the line. • • • •

With the running stitch, you can still see the line you drew as a guide. Use something that can be erased or washed away—like a chalk pencil, Wash-Away Stitch Stabilizer, or Sulky Sticky Fabri-Solvy.

Wendi says ...

Practice making all your stitches the same length. Then, practice breaking that rule! :-) Try longer stitches on top with shorter spaces between them. Or shorter stitches on top with longer spaces between them. Or vary long and short stitches. Play and make it fun!

Using a Hoop

Use a small embroidery hoop for most projects: 4"–7" across is a great size to work with.

1. Loosen the screw on the hoop to separate the 2 circles.

2. Place the smaller circle on a flat surface.

3. Lay your fabric over the smaller hoop, with the design centered in the circle.

4. Press the larger circle over the smaller circle, locking the fabric between the 2 rings. Tighten the screw a little, but not all the way.

5. Pull the fabric taut around the edges. It should be like a drum. After the fabric is taut and smooth, tighten the screw the rest of the way, as tight as you can get it.

Now you're ready to stitch.

backstitch

The backstitch is almost as easy as a running stitch. It gives you a nice solid line—perfect for outlining shapes.

1. Start just like the running stitch (page 41) by taking your first stitch.

2. Come up from the back, a stitch length away from the end of your first stitch. Pull the thread through to the front. ● ● ● ●

3. Instead of going forward a stitch, go backward. (See why they call it backstitch?) Put the needle through the same hole that ended the previous stitch. ● ● ●

4. Repeat Steps 2 and 3 until the end of the line. ● ● ●

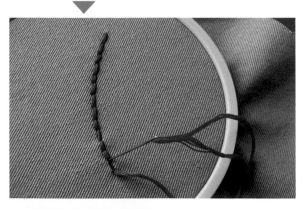

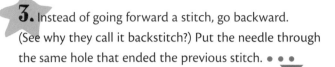

Wendi says ...

On the backstitch, I try to keep my stitches the same length—less than ¼". I think this looks neater. You might want to make your stitches a little smaller as you go around curves to make your curves look smoother.

lazy daisy stitch

This is a useful stitch to play with. It makes great flowers, of course, just as you'd expect with a name like lazy daisy. But it does so much more! It can become leaves, teardrops, insect wings, the knob at the end of an alien antenna, raindrops, scales. So many possibilities!

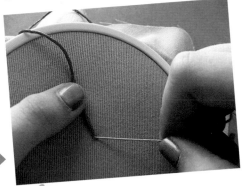

1. Thread your needle. Tie a knot in the end of the thread. Bring your thread up from the back, where you want the pointy end of your "drop" to be. Pull the thread through to the front.

2. Pull the needle down right next to where you came up. You can even go back in the same hole, but I usually move over a teeny bit.

3. Pull the thread most of the way through, but leave a floppy loop on the surface. ● ● ● ●

4. Needle up where you want the rounded end of your drop and go through the loop from Step 3. ● ● ● ●

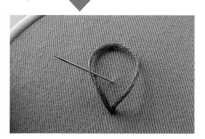

5. Pull the thread through to the front. The loop will tighten and the working thread will hold it in a nice curve. ● ● ● ●

6. Take a tiny stitch right over the curved end of the "drop." That will hold the whole thing in place. ● ● ● ●

Done!
So many possibilities!

french knot

A lot of people are afraid of French knots—but not you! There is nothing like French knots for peppering your work with tiny raised dots.

1. Thread your needle. Tie a knot in the end. Bring your thread up from the back where you want your dot.

2. The next few steps take both hands, so set down your hoop. Hold your working thread taut, but not too tight. With the needle pointing up *away from* the fabric, wrap the working thread once around the needle. ● ● ● ●
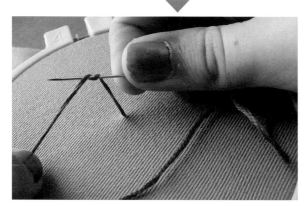

3. Holding everything tight, turn the needle so it points down into the fabric, near where you came up. Slide the thread wrap down the needle, so it's sitting on the fabric surface. ● ● ● ●

4. Use one finger to hold the working thread tight as you pull the needle through to the back of the fabric. ● ● ● ●
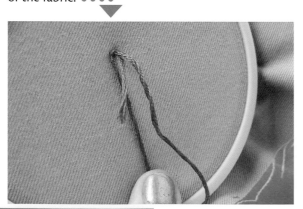

5. Pull the thread right through the thread wrap to make a nice little dimple in the surface of your knot.

Fancy, huh?

tall paul

MATERIALS

- ⅛ yard fabric (May I suggest cutting a leg off an old pair of jeans?)

- Embroidery thread

- #5 embroidery needle

- Embroidery hoop

- Printable stabilizer (such as Wash-Away Stitch Stabilizer or Sulky Sticky Fabri-Solvy)

- Chopstick

You pick the faces or draw your own and stack a totem pole as tall as you like.

make it

STITCH THE FRONT

1. Copy the faces you want to use on your totem pole, or draw your own. You can use the patterns on pages 48 and 49.

2. Print (or trace) the faces onto the bumpy side of a sheet of Sulky Sticky Fabri-Solvy.

3. Cut the faces apart and decide what order you want to stack them in.

The Skinny on Embroidery Thread

One of the nifty things about embroidery floss (not craft thread) is that you can choose how many strands to use. You can make your embroidered line as fat or as skinny as you like. Think of it as choosing a thick or a thin marker.

DMC embroidery floss comes in threads that are six strands thick. I often stitch with just four of those strands. Separating them is easy—if you know the trick.

1. Cut your thread the length you want. I usually use a length from my elbow to the tips of my fingers.

2. Hold your thread in the air so the whole length is dangling free.

3. From the top, tease out the number of strands you want to use. (But don't hurt their feelings. :-))

4. Slowly pull them free from the rest of the thread, letting the thread untwist as you go. It's important to go slowly and make sure your thread is always dangling free—not sitting in your lap.

Store the rest of your thread to use another time.

4. Peel off the paper backing. Stick the patterns onto the front of your fabric. Don't stick them near the edge of your fabric. Be sure to leave at least ½" all the way around for a seam allowance.

5. Hoop up your fabric so the first face you want to stitch is centered in your hoop (see page 41 for how to use an embroidery hoop).

6. Embroider the face right through the pattern and fabric. Use the backstitch or running stitch for the straight lines, the lazy daisy stitch for drop shapes, and French knots for dots. Jo used 4 strands of thread for all her stitching. ● ● ● ●

7. Keep moving your hoop as needed to embroider all your faces. When you are done, remove the hoop.

8. Fill up a sink with cool water. Swish your fabric through the water for a few minutes to dissolve the pattern/stabilizer. Roll the fabric up in a towel to squeeze out excess water. Lay it flat to dry.

MAKE THE TOTEM POLE

1. Cut out your pieces after your fabric is dry. Place 2 layers of fabric together and cut out a long rectangle, ½" bigger on all sides than your stitching. • • • ▶

2. Layer the fabric right sides together and pin all the way around.

3. Using ¼" seam allowance, sew the 2 layers together down a long side, across a short side, and down the other long side. Leave the other short side open for stuffing. Backstitch at the beginning and end.

4. Turn the totem pole right side out and use a chopstick to poke the corners out.

5. Turn in the raw edges of the opening and press. • ▶

6. Stuff it tightly, and then sew up the opening.

You pick the faces and stack a totem pole as tall as you like.

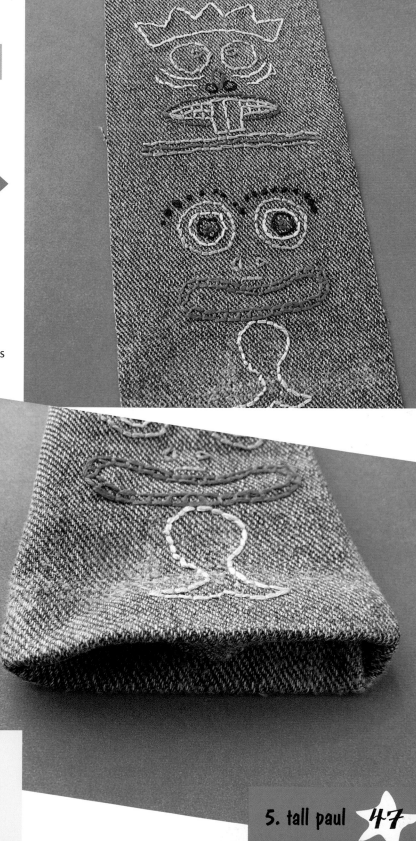

your turn!

What other kinds of faces can you stack in a totem pole?

Evelyn did this project without any embroidery at all. She drew all her faces with fabric markers—and she put faces on the front *and* back of her totem pole.

Now that you know how to embroider, you can go back and embroider the face on a robot pillow (page 25) instead of using the fabric markers. Or embroider eyes instead of using fusible adhesive.

6.

growing things out the seams

Words to Know

EMBELLISH: To add special stitching, appliqués, charms, or other decorations to your sewing project.

RICKRACK: A zigzag type of ribbon used to trim, decorate, and embellish items.

Now that you know how to sew and stuff a rectangle and different ways to add faces, let's talk about growing beyond that rectangle shape. Hair, arms, legs, tentacles, ridges, spikes—all of that can grow out of your softie, and seams are the easiest (and strongest) places to put them.

If you can sew through it, you can attach it to your softie. Rickrack, ribbon, and yarn all make good hair. Felt makes terrific arms and legs, hands and feet. But don't be limited to these items. Check out the trim section of a fabric store to see what you find. Fringes, beads, feathers—it's all good stuff! And don't just look at the fabric store. How about a bunch of rubber bands as hair? Or a tuft of the net bags that produce comes in? Think outside the box and see what you find!

The Number 1 rule of adding things to the seams of softies is to stay away from the corners! If any of your appendages get sewn into those corners, they'll get all twisted up and weird when you turn it right side out. So stay away!

Here's a quick biology lesson: An appendage is a body part—such as an arm, leg, tail, or fin—that is joined to the trunk (or main part) of a body. Felt is probably the easiest material to use for adding appendages. It comes in lots of terrific colors, and it doesn't fray, so you can cut exactly the shape you want and add it to the seam without any extra sewing. Use felt for flat arms, legs, tentacles, ears, and funky hair.

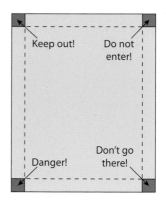

Keep out!   Do not enter!

Danger!   Don't go there!

1. Choose the shapes you want to use from the patterns on page 54.

2. Cut the shapes out of felt. Done! Well, not quite. You have to attach them to the softie now.

3. Place the softie front face up on a flat surface. Position the hair, arms, legs, etc., where you want them. Remember not to put anything in the corners! • • • • • • • • • • •

See how the yarn hair doesn't go all the way to the edges? That's because Jo is keeping it out of those corners.

4. Flip the appendages toward the softie, so they're face down and the edges are lined up with the raw edge of the softie front. Pin in place. • • • • • • • • • •

See how everything is flipped inside? The hair that will be growing up out of the top of the head is pointed down. And the legs that will be hanging down from the bottom of the body are pointed up.

SEAM ALLOWANCE PATROL

Make sure things are in the seam allowance only where you want them to be attached. The widest points of that dark green pointy bit that will be the feet are going to be a problem. See how they're coming almost all the way to the sides?

Fold them out of the way and hold them there with a bit of tape.

Now take a look at that purple spiral. See how close it's coming to the edges at the side and the top? Fold it out of the way so only the "stem" gets sewn into the seam.

Everything is neatly tucked away. The only things in the seam allowance are what you want sewn there.

You're ready!

5. Place the softie back so it is face down over the front, sandwiching the appendages between the layers. Pin in place. ● ● ● ● ● ▶

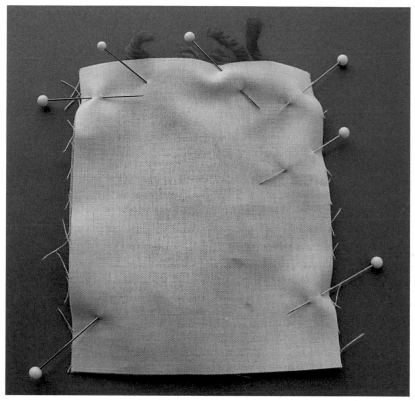

6. Sew the layers together. When using yarn, I like to sew across the seam at least twice. ● ● ● ● ▼

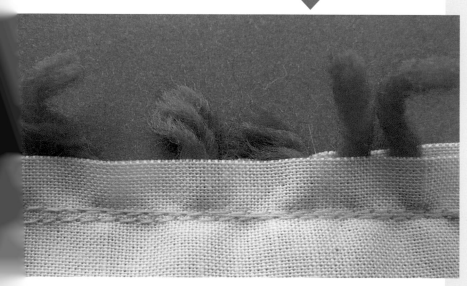

Leave 1"–2" for a stuffing opening! It can be at the top, side, or bottom—wherever you have room without appendages.

When you turn the softie right side out, all the appendages will be on the outside, securely attached at the seams.

creature camp

silly bean people

Finished size: 2½″ × 3¼″

MATERIALS

- Scraps of fabric
- Fabric markers, embroidery thread, or buttons for faces
- Yarn, rickrack, felt, and anything else cool you want to grow out of your little bean person
- Plastic pellets for stuffing
- Funnel

These little bean people are so much fun to make! Mix and match faces and appendages to make a huge assortment of them—no two have to be alike.

1. Transfer the face and body outline to a scrap of fabric. Use the patterns on page 58 or design your own!

2. Use markers to draw or embroidery thread to stitch the face. Add buttons for eyes if you like. ● ● ● ●
▼

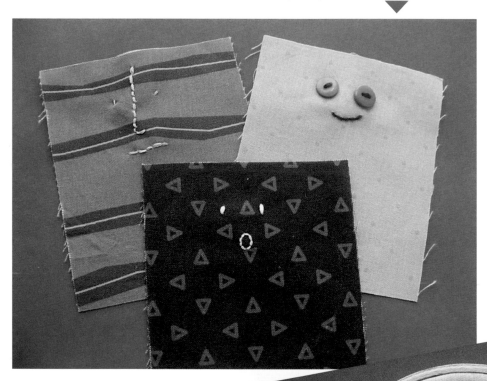

Use a small embroidery hoop for these small pieces, if needed.

3. Layer the body front with a second piece of fabric and cut out around both pieces at the same time.

4. Add whatever appendages (page 54) you choose. Don't forget to patrol your seam allowances! (See Seam Allowance Patrol on page 52.)

5. Sew the front to the back, with all the appendages sandwiched between them. Leave 1″–2″ open for stuffing.

6. Turn the bean person right side out and press the stuffing opening.

7. Insert a funnel into the stuffing opening and fill with 3–4 tablespoons of plastic pellets. Do *not* fill the body up to the top—you want the pellets to be loose so the body will be squishy.

The Silly Bean People say...

If you don't have a funnel, twist a piece of paper into a cone shape and make your own!

8. Sew up the stuffing opening.

9. Make another!

10. Repeat Step 9 as needed until you've made one for all your friends. :-)

creature camp

your turn!

Now that you know how to add things to the sides of your softies, what kinds of twists can you come up with for the first few projects? Want to try another robot pillow with an antenna coming out the top of his head? Or maybe a totem pole with wings growing out of the sides? Go for it!

Ivy made some wacky bean people with fabric markers, felt, and wildly patterned fabric.

Izzy used some super-simple shapes to turn her silly bean person into a sweet bear. Clever!

7.
getting
curvy

All right. We've done four projects that use only straight lines. It's time to start getting curvy. Just like we did with straight lines, I recommend you practice on some paper first.

1. Copy the curvy practice page (page 62).

2. Some of the curves are gentle and some are tight. Start with the gentle ones. They're *way* easier to handle.

3. Practice sewing right on the line. Then practice sewing ¼" away from the line. Keep practicing on the gentle lines.

4. Now move on to the tight curves. Yikes! These can be tricky. It feels like the sewing machine is going faster than you can steer the paper! Don't panic. Here are a few tips to help you with those tight curves.

- **Sew more slowly. Just easing up on the pedal will help a lot.** If your machine has speed control, use it.

- **Shorten your stitch length.** Newer machines will probably have a button to adjust your stitch length. Older machines might have a knob or lever. (See the diagram on page 8.) Read the manual to learn how to shorten the stitches on your machine. Then shorten them a little until the tight curves are easier to handle.

- **If all else fails, you can creep through a really tight section manually.** The technique is kind of similar to turning a corner. (Remember learning about that in Turning Corners on page 21?)

Wendi says ...

If you shorten your stitches to handle a curve, don't forget to lengthen them when you're done. Those teeny-tiny stitches are *not fun* to rip out if you make a mistake. Trust me.

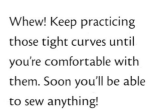

Here's how to make your way around that curve.

1. Sew right up to the tight curve. Stop. Use the handwheel to send your needle down into the fabric.

2. Leave the needle down and raise the presser foot. Spin the fabric just a bit, until you're lined up back on your curve.

3. Lower the presser foot and *slowly* sew another stitch or two. Sew as many stitches as you can before you feel like the curve is getting away from you. Then repeat Steps 1 and 2 to get back on track.

Whew! Keep practicing those tight curves until you're comfortable with them. Soon you'll be able to sew anything!

creature camp

clipping curves

Now that you're a master at sewing curves, you need to know a little trick about taking care of the seam allowance. Concave curves (the ones that curve in—like a cave) need to be clipped. You can sew the smoothest, most beautiful curve in the world, but if you don't clip the seam allowance, it will look awful when you turn it right side out. That's because the line of the cut edge of the fabric is shorter than the line of the stitched curve. The curve needs room to stretch out when you turn it. Give it that room by cutting little slits into the seam allowance. Be careful! You need to cut *right up to* the line of stitching, but don't cut *into* any of the stitches.

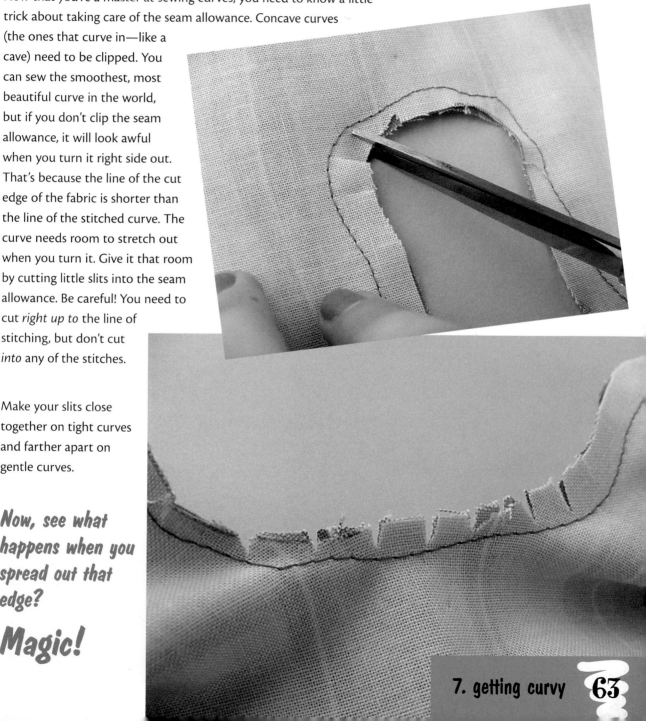

Make your slits close together on tight curves and farther apart on gentle curves.

Now, see what happens when you spread out that edge?

Magic!

clyde the curvy monster

Finished size: 8″ tall × 10″ wide (not counting those arms)

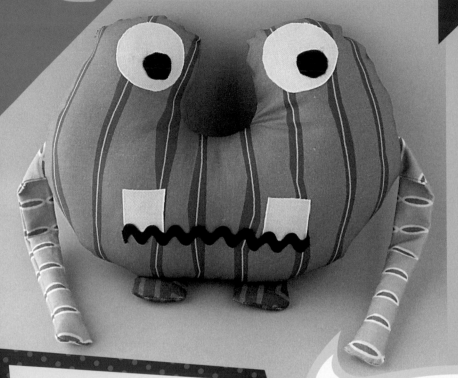

MATERIALS

- ¼ yard or 1 fat quarter patterned fabric
- Scraps of fabric for arms and feet
- Scraps of white fabric for eyes and teeth
- Fusible adhesive
- 2 buttons ⅝″ diameter or scraps of black felt for pupils
- 4″ black ribbon or rickrack for mouth
- Fiberfill stuffing
- Funnel
- Plastic pellets

Conquer concave curves and convex ones (the curves that round outward) with this curvy monster.

Clyde says …

The big white circles will help my eyes show up, no matter how patterned my body fabric is. So go crazy and choose something wild!

make it

PREP ALL THE PARTS

1. Cut out your fabric as instructed on the pattern pieces (pages 67 and 68). You're going to cut Clyde's body on the fold. Just fold the fabric in half (either direction, so the pattern goes the way you want) and line up the fold line on the pattern with the fold of your fabric.

2. Fold the arm rectangles in half the long way (right sides together) and sew across one of the short ends and down the long side. Backstitch at the beginning and end. Turn the arms right side out. Fill each with a tablespoon of plastic pellets. • • • ▼

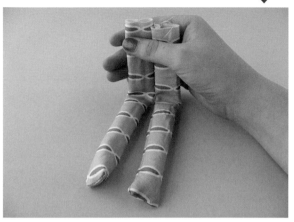

If you fill the arms all the way to the top, they'll be stiff. Fill them part way to make them floppy and pose-able.

3. For the feet, place 2 pieces right sides together. Sew down the sides and across the bottom. Leave the top open for stuffing. Stuff lightly. Repeat for the second foot. • • • ▼

See how Jo didn't stuff the foot all the way to the top? Just a pinch of stuffing is all you need.

Turning a Skinny Tube Right Side Out

Turning arms and legs right side out can be kind of tricky. There's a nifty tool available that makes it easy and fun. It's called Turn-it-All, a simple (and magical) set of tubes and sticks.

Here's how to use the tool:

1. Slide the tube part of the tool into the arm or leg, all the way to the end.

2. Poke a stick into the closed end of the arm or leg and then through the tube. • ▶

3. Keep pushing the stick into the tube. It will come out the other end—inside the arm or leg, which is now magically right side out. • • • • ▶

Fun, isn't it?

MAKE THE FACE

1. Use the white fabric and fusible adhesive to fuse the whites of the eyes and the teeth to the front monster piece. (See Glued on page 34 in Chapter 4 if you need a refresher on fusing.) Leave plenty of room around the eyes for the seam allowance. Add pupils using buttons or black felt. You can even use a marker to draw in the pupil. • • • •

2. Stitch the ribbon or rickrack in place for the mouth. • • •

PUT IT ALL TOGETHER

1. Place the monster front so it's face up on a flat surface. Arrange the arms and feet where you like them. Flip them to the inside of the monster and pin them in place. • • •

2. Place the monster back piece so it's face down over the front. Pin the 2 layers together so the arms and feet are sandwiched between them.

Using ¼" seam allowance, sew the 2 layers together, leaving about 4" open for stuffing. Don't forget to back-stitch at the beginning and end of your sewing. • • • ▼

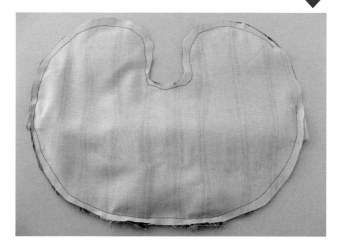

3. The curve between the monster's eyes is concave, so it needs to be clipped. Snip right up to, but not into, your stitching line.

4. Turn your monster right side out. Press under the raw edges of the stuffing opening.

5. Stuff your monster so he's smooth and round, with no wrinkles or dips.

6. Stitch the stuffing opening closed.

Give him a big hug.

Clyde
Arm
Cut 2.

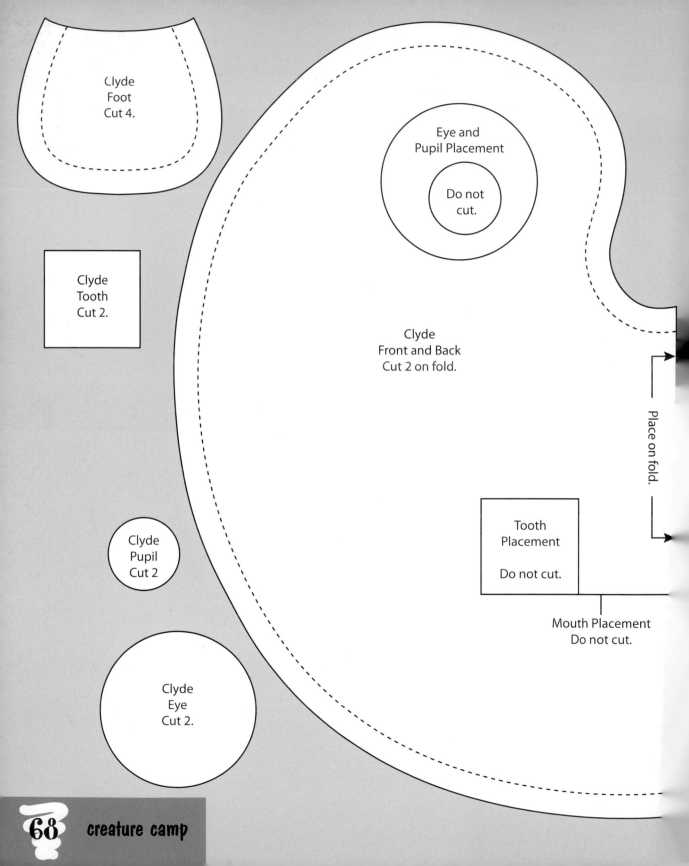

Clyde
Foot
Cut 4.

Clyde
Tooth
Cut 2.

Eye and
Pupil Placement

Do not
cut.

Clyde
Front and Back
Cut 2 on fold.

Place on fold.

Tooth
Placement

Do not cut.

Clyde
Pupil
Cut 2

Mouth Placement
Do not cut.

Clyde
Eye
Cut 2.

your turn!

Now that you know how to sew curves, take another look at the projects you've already done. Make a round robot head. Enlarge your favorite eye pattern and make an eye-shaped pair of pillows. Make bean-shaped bean people. Go ahead—get curvy!

Lillian made a furry Clyde. You'll learn how to use furry fabrics in Chapter 17 (page 136). She also swapped his arms and legs so he has itty-bitty stubby arms and loooong skinny legs. Cute!

How will you put your own spin on this pattern? Will you change the shape of the eyes or give it pointy teeth? Maybe give it long, dangly arms *and* legs. Make it two-sided with a different face on the back. Play!

8.
tails, fairy wings, and things

What if you want something growing out of your softie, such as a tail, which would not grow out of a side seam? Well, you can add more seams! Add an extra seam to the back of a softie for that tail or for fairy wings or some back ridges. Add a seam between the head and the body to add a collar or a neck ruff. Add a seam at the back of the head to give your creature a ponytail. Oh, the many possibilities!

prairie points

Prairie points are one of my favorite things to add to these extra seams. A prairie point is a special kind of flat triangle that doesn't need any sewing. You just need a square of fabric and some time with the iron. These points make excellent crowns, ears, back ridges, noses, and other pointy flat extras. And they're easy!

1. Cut a square of fabric.

2. Fold it in half on the diagonal. Press. • • • •

3. Fold it in half again on the other diagonal so the raw edges meet. Press. • • • •

Done!

The raw edges are now all on one side, and that's the side you sew into the seam. The nifty way these are folded allows you to nest them together nicely. • • • • • • • ▶

gus the grinning gator

Finished size: 14″ long × 4″ wide

MATERIALS

- ⅛ yard dark green fabric for back
- ⅛ yard light green fabric for belly
- Scraps of green fabric for back ridges
- Scraps of white fabric for eyes
- Scraps of felt for feet
- Black fabric marker or small buttons

Gus says ...

Gators are dark green on top and light green on the belly. That helps us blend into our surroundings, so we can sneak up on our prey. Snap! Yum, yum. Dinner! :-) If you choose to use a color other than green, stick to the dark-on-the-top, light-on-the-bottom color combo for a more realistic look.

An alligator is able to float beneath the surface of the water with just his eyes and a few back ridges visible. We're going to mimic that ability with our alligator softie.

So far everything we've made has used two main pattern pieces—a front and a back. This time we're going to add two extra seams. We will put the first one between the head and the body, so we can have sneaky eyes that pop above the water line. The second seam will go down the center of the back and tail, so we can have some ridges standing up.

make it

1. Cut out all the fabric as it says on the pattern pieces (pages 75 and 76).

Gus says ...

You'll notice there's no pattern piece for my belly. That's not a mistake. You'll make the top of my body and then use that finished piece to cut my belly. So for the gator head and body, use the fabric you want seen on top. For example, I have a dark green head and body.

2. Make the eyes. Place a white piece and a green piece right sides together and sew them together around the curved edge, using ¼" seam allowance. Don't forget to backstitch at the beginning and end of your stitching. Repeat for the second eye. • • •

3. Turn the eyes right side out and put a tiny pinch of stuffing inside. You don't want them to be stuffed tight—just a little bit puffy. • • •

4. Fold the squares into prairie points (page 71) for the back ridges.

MAKE THE GATOR BACK

1. Line up the prairie points along the straight line on the alligator back pieces. Stay out of the ¼" zone on each end! You'll need to overlap the prairie points a tiny bit to get them to fit. Pin it all in place. • • •

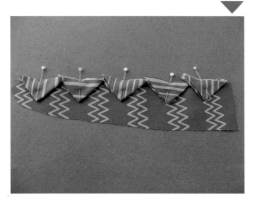

2. Place the second back pattern piece over the front, right side down, sandwiching the prairie points between them. Pin in place. Sew that straight seam, using ¼" seam allowance. • • •

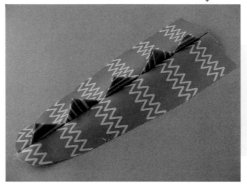

See how those ridges stand up?

3. Position an eye on each side of the ridges. Place the green side of the eye down. Pin in place. • • • •

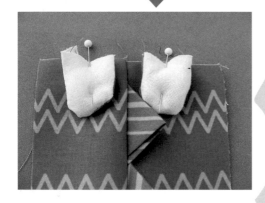

4. Place the head so that it is face down over the body piece, with the eyes sandwiched between the 2 layers. Pin in place.

5. Sew the head to the body using a ¼" seam allowance.

6. Unfold the gator back. This is your pattern piece for the gator belly. ▸

PUT IT ALL TOGETHER

1. Smooth the gator back completely. Trace around it onto the belly fabric. Cut out the alligator belly.

2. Position the alligator feet on the sides of the body. Place 2 feet right behind the eyes and the other 2 about halfway between the first feet and the tip of the tail. Pin in place. ● ● ●

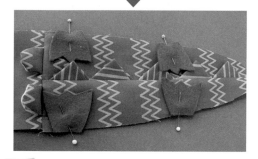

3. Layer the alligator belly over the alligator top, right side down, and pin in place, sandwiching the feet between the layers. ● ● ● ● ▶

4. Using ¼″ seam allowance, stitch the layers together, leaving the space between 2 of the feet open for stuffing. Don't forget to backstitch at the beginning and end.

5. Turn the alligator right side out. Neatly press the seam allowance of the stuffing opening.

6. Stuff the alligator. Be sure to work from each end to the opening in the center.

7. Sew the stuffing opening closed.

8. Use a fabric marker to add a fat pupil to the center of each eye.

He's finished!

Gator
Head
Cut 1.

Gator
Ridge
Cut 5.

Gator
Body
Cut 2.

Gator
Eye
Cut 2 white.
Cut 2 green.

Gator
Foot
Cut 4 from felt.

your turn!

If you want to give your alligator a toothy grin, hand stitch white rickrack over the seam between the top of the head and the bottom. Fun!

Liam made his alligator exactly as the pattern described— but he used funky purple fabrics. I love it! It makes me wish there really were purple alligators out there!

9.
getting more curvy

In Chapter 8 (page 70), we learned that you could add extra seams to your softie to attach parts such as eyeballs and back ridges. So far you've used straight seams to anchor those parts. But if you curve those seams, you can give your softie more shape.

Sew these seams the same way you sewed curvy side seams in Chapter 7 (page 60). Things will start to look weird when you put the front and back together, because the front and back pieces won't always be flat anymore. Just be patient and keep going. And use plenty of pins!

harry the round-bellied bear

Finished size: *6″ × 8″*

MATERIALS

- ¼ yard fabric or 1 fat quarter
- Scrap of felt for nose
- 2 safety eyes, 9mm
- Fabric marker for mouth
- Fiberfill stuffing

We're getting even curvier with this round-bellied bear. He's so huggable!

Harry says ...

Choose a fabric without much pattern so you can see my face. If my body fabric is light, use dark eyes, felt, and thread or markers. If my body fabric is dark, use light eyes, felt, and thread for the face. Not many markers show up on dark fabric, so embroidering is the best choice for dark fabric.

make it

PREP ALL THE PARTS

1. Cut out the pattern pieces as directed on pages 83 and 84. Cut a small triangle out of felt for the nose.

2. Place 2 ears right sides together. Using ¼" seam allowance, sew them together around the sides and bottom. Backstitch at the beginning and end. Repeat for the other ear and for the hands and feet.

Harry says ...

If you want me to have puffy ears and paws instead of flat ones, skip the pressing in Step 3. Instead, add a tiny pinch of stuffing to each piece.

3. Turn an ear right side out. Smooth it out and press. Repeat for the other ear and the hands and feet. ● ● ● ●▶

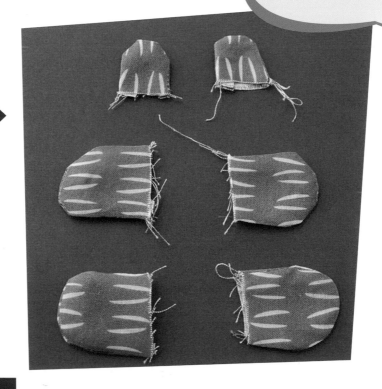

GIVE HIM A FACE

1. Place the front pieces with right sides together. Using ¼" seam allowance, sew down the center front line. • • • • • ▶

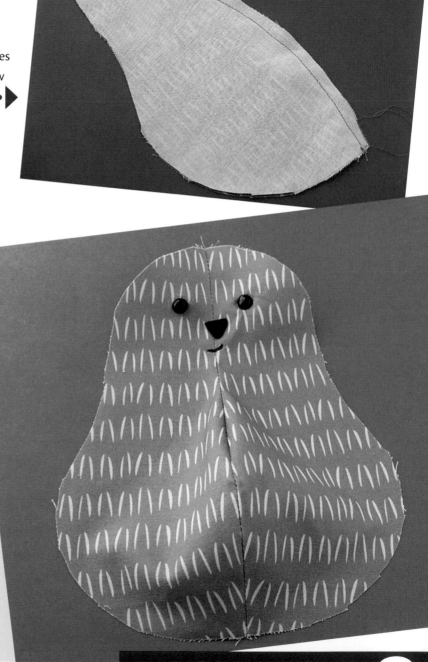

2. Add a face. This one has safety eyes, a felt nose, and a mouth drawn on with a fabric marker. You can switch out any of those you like. Use button eyes or stitched eyes. Draw on all the features with a fabric marker. Embroider them all with thread. Make it the way you like it. • • • • • • • • • ▶

Give it the *personality* you want it to have!

PUT IT ALL TOGETHER

1. Place the bear's front face up on a flat surface. Position the ears and paws and pin them in place. ● ● ● ●
▼

2. Fold the bear's back piece in half and mark the center top and bottom points with pins.

3. Place the front piece face down on the back, with the ears and paws sandwiched between the layers. Line up the center front seam with the pins at the top and bottom. Pin the layers together. ● ● ● ●
▼

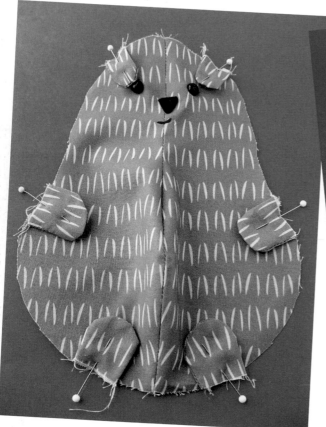

4. Using ¼″ seam allowance, sew all the way around the bear, leaving a few inches open above a bear hand for stuffing. Backstitch at the beginning and end.

5. Clip the inside curves at the sides, where the bear's neck dips in.

6. Turn the bear right side out. Neatly press the seam allowance of your stuffing opening.

7. Stuff. Stitch the opening closed.

Bear
Back
Cut 1 on fold.

Place on fold.

Bear
Hand and Foot
Cut 8.

Bear
Ear
Cut 4.

Bear
Front
Cut 2.

Ready for a challenge? Make the round-bellied bear into a round-bellied *and* round-bottomed bear. Don't use the bear back pattern piece. Instead, cut another two bear front pieces. Join them and use them for the back piece. Easy peasy!

Alicia didn't use the bear ear pattern. Instead she drew her own pattern for big floppy ears, which turned her bear into a bunny! Fabulous!

10.
having
a ball

You can make a few simple shapes
by making one section and then
repeating it a set number of times.
The trick to these shapes is not to
sew into the seam allowance.

The pattern pieces for the next few projects are marked with large dots at the places where you should start and stop stitching. Transfer the dots to your fabric pieces so you can see them when you're sewing. Here's how to do it.

You can make a few simple shapes by making one section and then repeating it a set number of times.

1. Cut out your fabric piece. Place it face up on a hard surface.

2. Place your pattern piece on top of the fabric piece with the edges lined up.

3. Stick a pin through the dot on the pattern piece and into the fabric piece beneath it.

4. Flip over the pattern and fabric. Make a dot where the pin is sticking out of the fabric. • • • •

5. Repeat these steps for the rest of the dots on your pattern pieces. These are the places where you'll start and stop all your stitching. • • • •

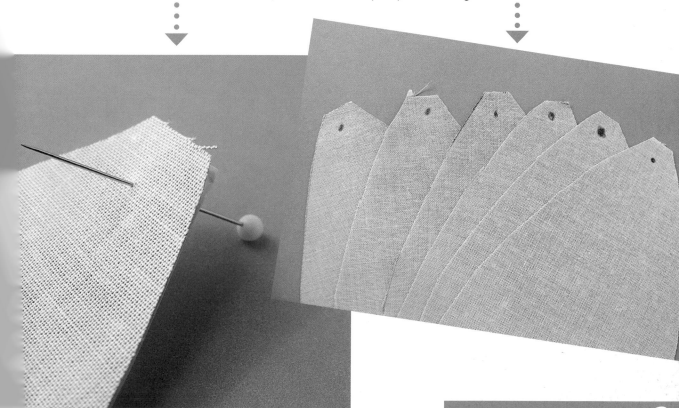

percy the round piggy

Finished size: 6″ wide × 6″ high

MATERIALS

- ¼ yard fabric or 1 fat quarter
- 1 fat pipe cleaner or chenille stem
- 1 button, 1½″ diameter
- 2 safety eyes, 9mm
- Fiberfill stuffing

Percy says ...

Choose a fabric that doesn't have a bold print so that you can see my eyes. But don't limit yourself to pink. Make me in muddy brown or funky bright colors! I've even seen green pigs in a video game. :-)

Six football-shaped wedges make a perfect round ball. We're inserting ears and a tail into the seams to turn that ball into a round piggy.

make it

PREP ALL THE PARTS

1. Cut out all the fabric as it says on the pattern pieces (page 92). Transfer the dots onto each wedge so you know where to start and stop your stitching.

2. Place 2 ear pieces right sides together. Sew them together on 2 sides, leaving the third side open for turning. Turn the ear right side out and press it flat. Repeat this step for the other ear. ● ● ● ● ● ➤

3. Fold the tail in half the long way, right sides together. Sew across one short side and down the long side. Backstitch at the beginning and end of your stitching. Turn the tail right side out. Slide the pipe cleaner all the way up into the tail. ● ● ▶

4. Trim off the excess pipe cleaner.

PUT THE BELLY TOGETHER

1. Place 2 wedges right sides together and pin. Sew one side together (only one side!) from dot to dot, backstitching at the beginning and end.

Percy says ...

What if after sewing, you flip your wedges over and the stitching didn't end on the bottom dot?

Don't worry. Fabric is bendy and flexible. Sometimes things just don't line up. I'm still going to look great.

2. Add a third wedge to the group, pinning it to one side of the first pair. Be sure the seam allowance from Step 1 is out of the way. As you sew the new seam from dot to dot, you should only be sewing through 2 layers. ● ● ● ● ● ● ● ▶

You should end up with what looks like an empty bowl. This is the bottom half of the pig. Sewing the top half together will be almost just like it, except we'll also be sewing the ears into 2 seams.

See how the seam allowance and the first wedge are pushed over to the right and out of the way?

PUT THE TOP TOGETHER

1. Fold the ears in half. • • • • • • • • • • ▶

2. Position them on both sides of a wedge about halfway between the tip of the wedge and its widest point. • • ▶

3. Layer a second wedge face down over the first, with the ears sandwiched between them. Sew from dot to dot, catching an ear in the stitching. Backstitch at the start and end of your stitching.

4. Add a third wedge, this time catching the other ear in the seam.

Now you should have 2 empty bowls: a piggy top and bottom. • • • ▶

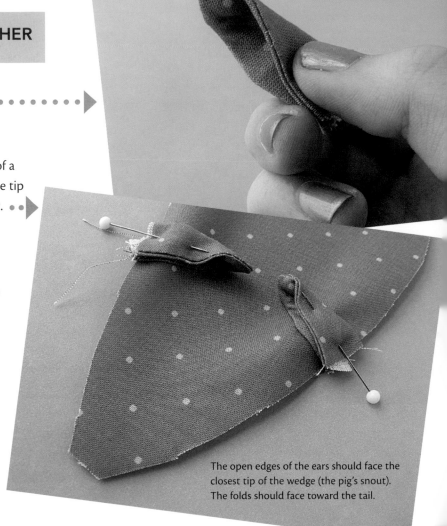

The open edges of the ears should face the closest tip of the wedge (the pig's snout). The folds should face toward the tail.

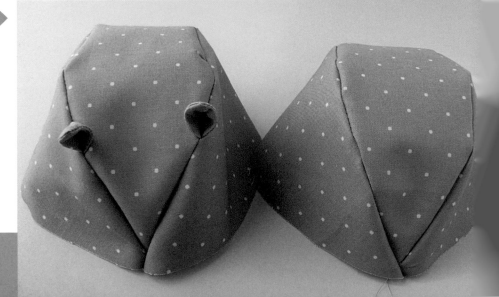

PUT IT ALL TOGETHER

1. Pin the tail to the piggy top, right where all 3 wedges come together in the back. • • • •

2. Turn the bottom bowl inside out. Layer it together with the first bowl, with the tail sandwiched between the 2 layers and right sides together. Pin the bowls together, leaving 4"–5" open for stuffing in the middle of a side seam. You'll need a wider opening because you'll be sewing a button through the opening and attaching safety eyes. Give yourself room to work. • • •

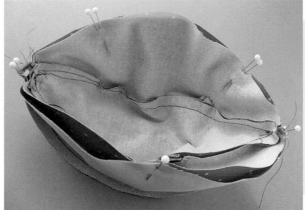

See how large the stuffing opening is? It's the space between the double pins.

3. Sew the 2 bowls together.

4. Turn the pig right side out. Neatly press the raw edges of the stuffing opening.

5. Sew a large button on the front where all the seams come together. This is the nose.

6. Attach 2 safety eyes halfway between the nose and the ears, just to the outside of the seams between the ears and the nose. • • • •

7. Stuff. Sew the stuffing opening closed. Twirl the tail into a nice corkscrew. You're done! ▶

10. percy the round piggy **91**

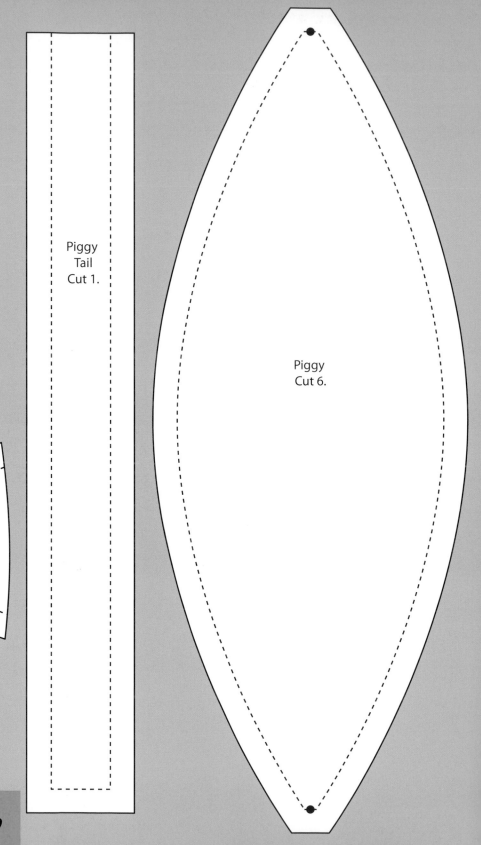

Piggy
Tail
Cut 1.

Piggy
Ear
Cut 4.

Piggy
Cut 6.

creature camp

What else can you make from a sphere? A ball, of course! Leave off the ears and tail. Make each wedge a different color for a rainbow ball.

FUN!
What else can you make?

Jo made a furry ball and turned it into a monster by adding a couple of safety eyes to one side.

11.
get to
the point

In Chapter 10, we learned to make a round shape by sewing wedges together from dot to dot. We were careful to stay out of the seam allowances. Now we're going to take that skill a step further by using it to make corners.

Sewing two pieces of fabric together from dot to dot is easy. The trick is when you add a third (or fourth) piece to come together in a corner. You'll have to fold your seam allowance out of the way. After you pin your pieces together, be sure to do another check from dot to dot to make sure you're only ever sewing through two layers of fabric at a time. If your seam allowances have flipped into the area you want to stitch, pin them back out of the way.

creature camp

peabody the penguin

Finished size: 5″ × 5″

MATERIALS

- 3 scraps of black fabric for back and bottom
- Scrap of white fabric for belly
- Scrap of orange fabric for feet
- Fiberfill stuffing

Four equilateral triangles make a triangle-based pyramid. Add a couple of prairie points (page 71) for feet, and you have a penguin. Squint. It really is a penguin. I thought you had an imagination! :-)

make it

PREP ALL THE PARTS

1. Cut 3 black triangles, 1 white triangle, and 2 orange squares using the pattern pieces on page 98. Transfer the dots at the points of all the triangles, as you learned on page 87.

2. Fold the orange squares into prairie points (page 71).

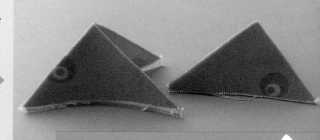

BUILD THE PYRAMID

1. Fold the white triangle in half. Mark the center point of the base with a pin. Position the 2 orange triangles on either side of that center pin. Pin in place. ● ● ● ●

See the pin marking the center? The tips of the 2 prairie points touch at that pin.

2. Place a black triangle face down over the white triangle, with the feet sandwiched between the layers. Pin in place. Sew the 2 triangles together on the side with the feet, sewing from dot to dot. Backstitch at the beginning and end. ● ● ● ●

3. Now you're ready to add another triangle. Layer a second black triangle over the first one. Sew them together from dot to dot. This side will have the stuffing opening in it, so leave an opening of about 2″ right in the middle. Backstitch at the beginning and end, as well as on both ends of the stuffing hole. ● ●

Peabody says ...

When you start adding more pieces, it's easy to make a mistake lining them up. You need to line up each piece with the *edges* of the piece underneath it, *not with the seams*. Look ...

The new piece (the one with the dot showing) is lined up wrong. The up-and-down edge is lined up with the seam below it—not with the cut edge of the fabric. See those triangles sticking out of the top? I call them bunny ears. Use them to help you line things up. The point of this new triangle is sitting below the bunny ears—not lined up with either of them. ● ● ● ●

In this picture, the piece is lined up correctly. The new triangle is shifted over so that it's lined up with the left bunny ear. That puts the dot right over the seam below it—perfect. ● ● ● ● ● ● ● ● ● ● ● ● ●

4. Attach the fourth triangle to the other side of the white triangle. Sew from dot to dot. Press the seam open. The triangles will all line up in a row, making a parallelogram (a four-sided flat shape with opposite sides parallel.) ● ● ● ●

5. Start folding up the pieces. Fold the row of triangles so the belly piece is folded in half and 2 black triangles are lined up at the top edge. Pin the seam allowances out of the way. Sew from dot to dot. ● ● ● ● ● ● ● ● ● ● ● ● ● ● ● ● ●

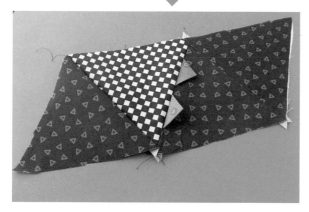

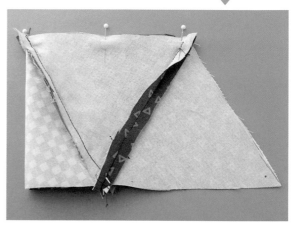

6. Sewing the first 3-D seam will make your toy look like a cave with a triangle flap at the opening. ● ● ● ● ● ● ● ● ●

Fold up that last flap. Stitch the 2 remaining seams. Remember to only stitch from dot to dot. Backstitch at the beginning and end of each seam. Don't try to turn a 3-D corner like this. Instead, sew the first seam, backstitch, and take it out of the machine. Line up the next seam and sew it in a separate run through the machine.

7. Turn your penguin right side out. Use a chopstick to push each point out neatly. Fill the points with stuffing first and then stuff the middle. Stuff it loosely so it feels kind of like a marshmallow.

8. Stitch up the opening. You're done!

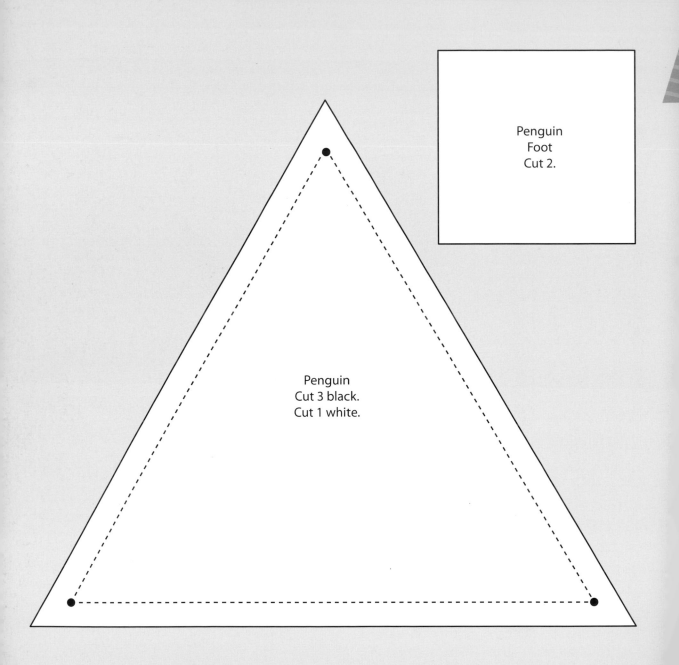

Penguin
Foot
Cut 2.

Penguin
Cut 3 black.
Cut 1 white.

your turn!

When I first developed this idea, I tried to see how simple it could be but still look like a creature. Haley made a chick by using yellow triangles for the body and an orange prairie point for the beak. Can you see it?

Use dark green on the back and bottom, light green on the belly, and add a row of prairie points down the back to make a dinosaur. Do the same thing with purples and call it a dragon. What other kinds of animals can you make out of a pyramid? It's amazing what you can make with a few triangles and some imagination!

12.
what a bunch of squares!

That pyramid in Chapter 11 is an example of a 3-D (three-dimensional) form called a regular tetrahedron. Each face is the exact same shape. If you were really ambitious, you could go to crazy extremes making these forms. How about a dodecahedron with 20 pentagons? No? That's okay; I really don't recommend it. :-) We're going to stick with a six-sided shape that you can have fun with—a cube.

roland the die

Finished size: 6″ square

MATERIALS

- ¼ yard fabric or 1 fat quarter
- 21 buttons, 1″
- Fiberfill stuffing

Six squares make a perfect cube. Add colorful buttons and you have a squishy die. Make two and you have a pair of dice. (Isn't it weird that one is called a die?)

make it

PREP ALL THE PARTS

1. Using the pattern on page 104, cut 6 squares. Transfer the dots at the corners of the pattern to each square, as you learned on page 87.

2. Sew the buttons on the square so they look like the sides of a die. Remember that ¼″ around each square will be in the seam allowance, so don't put the buttons too close to the edge.

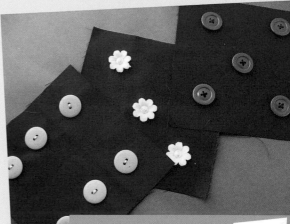

PUT IT ALL TOGETHER

1. Place the 1- and 2-button pieces right sides together. Sew them together *from dot to dot only*, using ¼″ seam allowance. Leave a 2″–3″ opening in the middle of the seam for stuffing. Don't forget to backstitch at the beginning and end. ● ● ● ▶

Press the raw edges of the opening flat so you have a nice clean edge to stitch closed.

2. Add the 6-button piece to the other side of the 2-button piece. ● ● ● ● ● ● ● ● ● ● ● ● ● ● ● ▶

3. Add the 5-button piece to the other side of the 6-button piece. You should have a row of 4 squares sewn together.

Be careful to keep the seam allowance out of the stitching. See how it's folded back away from the area to be stitched? The stitching will go right up to where the pin is but through only two layers of fabric.

4. Sew the 3-button piece to the top of the 2-button piece. Remember—sew only from dot to dot and backstitch at the start and finish.

5. Sew the 4-button piece to the remaining side of the 2-button piece. You should now have a flat cross shape. ● ● ● ● ● ● ● ● ● ● ▶

6. Time to start folding those sides into a cube! This will involve a little fancy folding, but remember—you're sewing only from dot to dot, so that's what should be lined up and smooth. The rest of the cube can be a wadded up mess; only worry about the 2 sides you're working on.

Sew the side of the 3-button piece to the top of the 1-button piece. You'll need to fold the 2-button piece in half on the diagonal to keep it out of the way. • • • • • • • • • • • • • • • • •

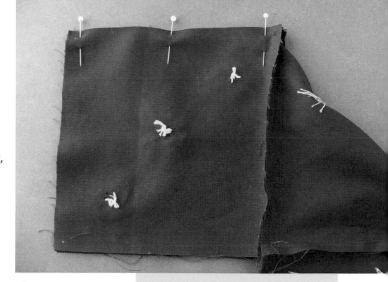

See how that works?

7. Continue around the rest of the cube, sewing up sides from dot to dot until you have an inside-out cube. • •▶

8. Turn the cube right side out. Use a chopstick or similar tool to push out the corners.

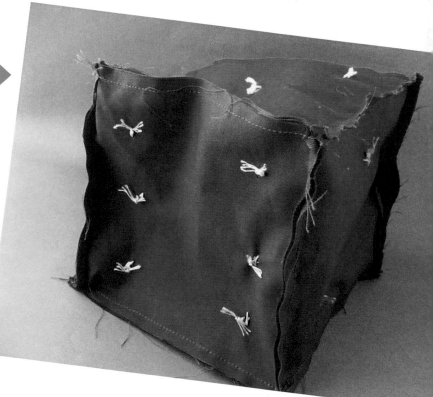

9. Stuff it neatly. Get some stuffing into all the corners before you stuff the middle; otherwise, you'll have more of a round shape than a cube.

10. Sew up the opening. Roll your die.

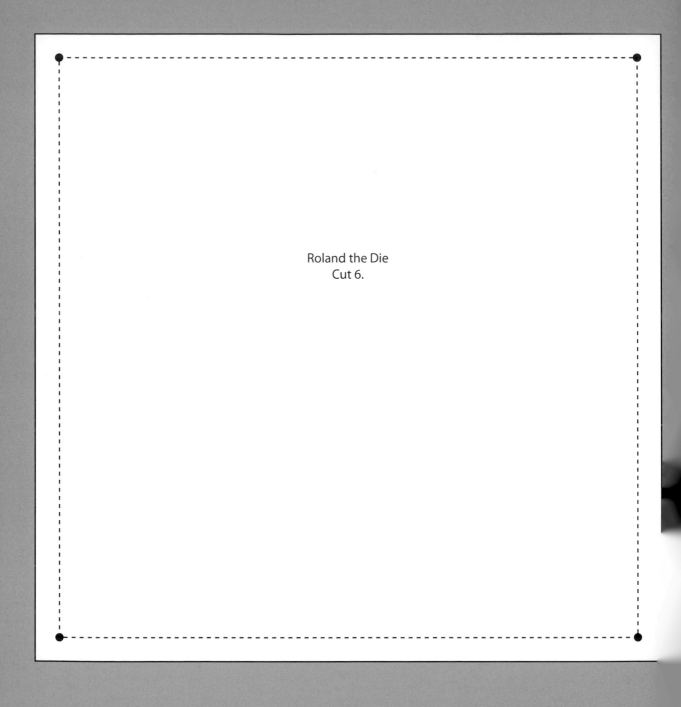

Roland the Die
Cut 6.

creature camp

your turn!

Do you need to make another one for a pair? How about varying each side? Use fabric markers to draw six different faces with different emotions on each side. Or add six pairs of spooky eyes using the eye patterns from Chapter 4 (page 38).

Sharon turned her cube into a cat! She drew the face with fabric markers and used two cat safety eyes. She folded squares into two prairie points (page 71) for the ears. She made a long, skinny tail filled with pellets so it would swing nicely. Cute!

What other kinds of animals can you make out of a cube?

13.
fat is good: adding a gusset

A gusset is a piece of fabric added to a project to make part of it wider. In softies, gussets are often used to make the top of a head wider than the jaw or to add width to the bottom of an animal. We're going to use one to take a flat hen and make her a fat hen.

First take a look at the pattern pieces on the next page.

We could easily sew those two main body pieces together, turn them right side out, stuff them, and have a hen. But she would be flat and would lie on her side. That's great for a hanging ornament but not for a softie. We're going to add that football-shaped gusset to give her belly a base, so she'll sit up and look plump.

The process is just like sewing the geometric shapes you did in the previous chapters. This time the shapes aren't identical—but you're still sewing from dot to dot and staying out of the seam allowances.

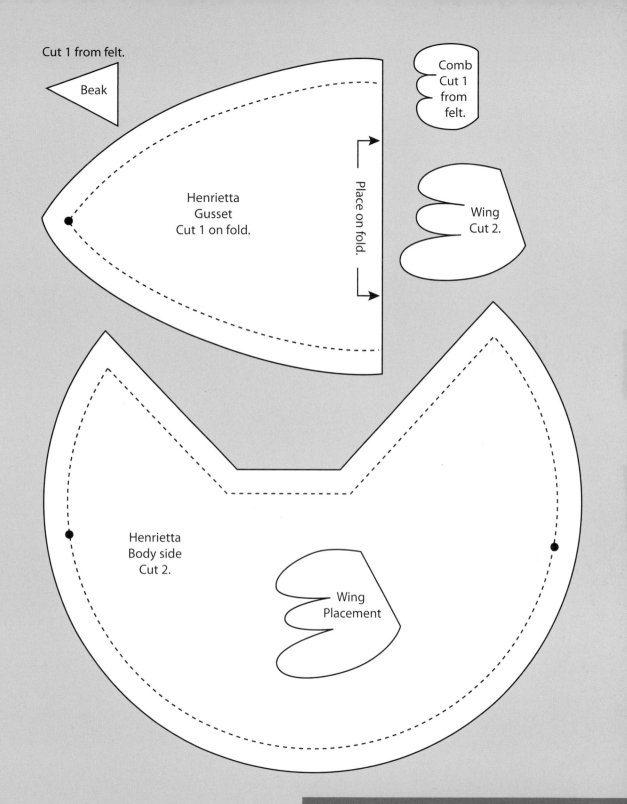

Cut 1 from felt.

Beak

Henrietta
Gusset
Cut 1 on fold.

Place on fold.

Comb
Cut 1
from
felt.

Wing
Cut 2.

Henrietta
Body side
Cut 2.

Wing
Placement

henrietta the hen

Finished size: 5″ long × 3″ wide × 4″ tall

MATERIALS

- ¼ yard fabric
- Scrap of fabric for wings
- Fusible adhesive
- Scraps of felt for beak and comb
- Fiberfill stuffing

This little hen won't lay any eggs, but she'll sure look sweet sitting in your lap. And she'll never peck you!

make it

PREP ALL THE PARTS

1. Cut 2 body pieces and a gusset from your main fabric, using the pattern on page 107. Transfer the dots to your fabric. Cut a comb (the "crown" on the head, usually red in real life). Cut a beak from felt scraps.

2. Attach the wings to the body with fusible adhesive. (See Glued on page 34 if you need a refresher.)
••••••••••→

Henrietta says ...

I don't have any eyes, so you don't have to worry about whether they'll show up on the body fabric you choose. Go ahead and choose something wild! Just make sure what you choose for my wings contrasts well with my body.

PUT IT ALL TOGETHER

1. Position the comb and the beak where you want them. Flip them to the inside. Line up the fabric edges. Pin in place. ▶

2. Layer the second body piece over the first, right sides together, with the comb and beak sandwiched between them. Sew the sides of the body together using ¼″ seam allowance, sewing from dot to dot around the top of the body. Don't forget to backstitch at the dots.

3. Snip into the corners at the hen's back. ••••••••▶

Cut right up to, but not into, the line of stitching.

4. Slip the gusset into place, so that one dot lines up with the dot at the front of the body and the other dot lines up with the dot at the back. Pin the gusset to the body. Sew from the front dot to the back dot, backstitching at the dots. • • • • • • ▼

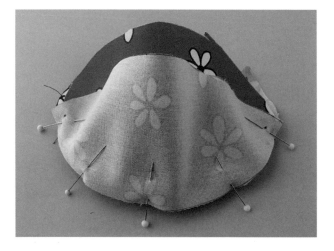

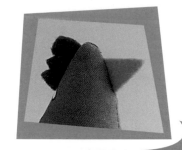

Henrietta says ...

Sometimes pinning curves can be tricky. Start by pinning at each dot. Next pin the middle of the curves together. Then add two more pins between the center and dot pins.

5. Take the fabric out of the machine. Rearrange things so you're sewing the other side of the gusset to the other side of the body. Pin the layers together. Mark a 3″–4″ opening for the stuffing. Sew from one dot to the start of the stuffing opening. Then sew from the end of the stuffing opening to the other dot. Make sure that the seam allowances are out of the way and you're sewing through only 2 layers. Don't forget to backstitch every time you start and stop sewing.

6. Turn your hen right side out. Neatly press the stuffing opening. Stuff the head and tail first, then the body. Sew the opening closed. Give her a squeeze.

Make a whole flock of hens in a rainbow of colors!

Sophia added legs to her chicken! She made two tubes of fabric for the legs (page 65) and then added a seam (page 70) to the middle of the gusset piece so that she had a place to attach the legs.

Do you want to do it, too? Add ¼" seam allowance to the fold line of the gusset pattern piece. Cut 2 pieces instead of 1 on the fold.

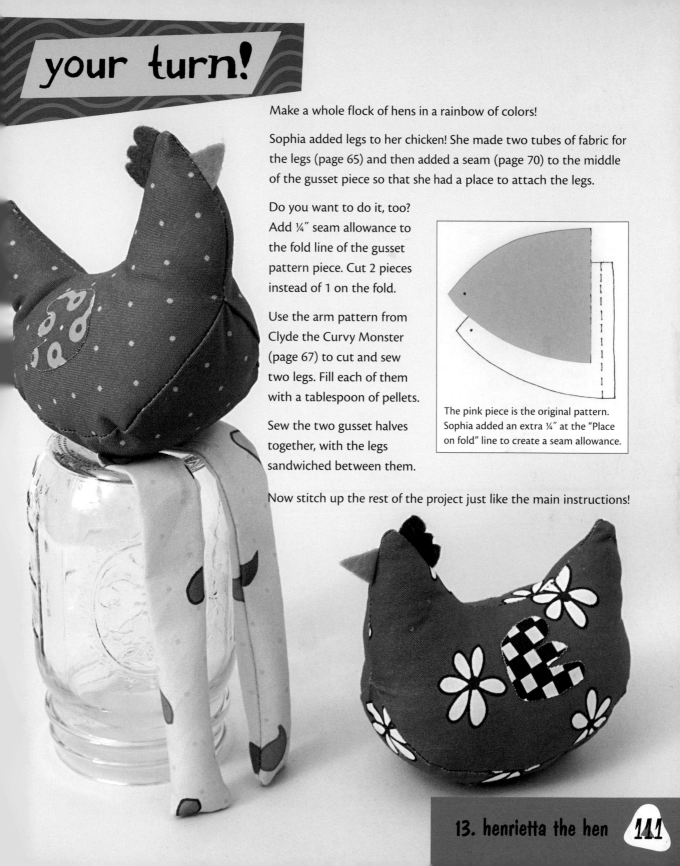

Use the arm pattern from Clyde the Curvy Monster (page 67) to cut and sew two legs. Fill each of them with a tablespoon of pellets.

Sew the two gusset halves together, with the legs sandwiched between them.

The pink piece is the original pattern. Sophia added an extra ¼" at the "Place on fold" line to create a seam allowance.

Now stitch up the rest of the project just like the main instructions!

14.
fancy
stuffing

Everything we've made so far has used either fiberfill stuffing or plastic pellets. You can pack fiberfill very tightly for a firm softie or leave it fairly loose and fluffy for a squishy softie. Pellets always need to be filled loosely so that you get that special beanie feel. Did you know that you can combine all three stuffing methods (firm stuffing, loose stuffing, and pellet stuffing) in a single softie? Oh yes!

The most common way to use this method is by packing the arms, legs, and other appendages tightly with stuffing, while leaving the stuffing in the body squishy and soft. It works best when the arms or legs have kind of skinny attachments. That way, when you pack the stuffing, it tends to stay in place, instead of working its way back into the main softie body.

wallace the whale

Finished size: 8″ long × 5″ tall × 3″ wide

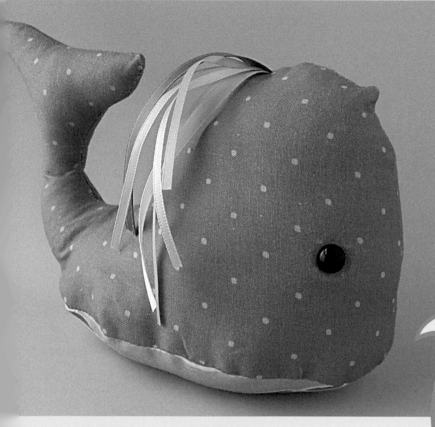

MATERIALS

- ¼ yard fabric or 1 fat quarter for main body

- Scrap of fabric for belly

- 2 eyes (buttons, safety eyes, stitched eyes, or fabric marker—you choose)

- Ribbon scraps (Jo used 6 strips, each about 4½″ long.)

- Fiberfill stuffing

- Plastic pellets

Wallace says ...

Most marine animals are dark on top and light on the bottom. So if you want me to look more real, choose a lighter fabric for my belly. And make sure to use a main fabric that will let my eyes show up. I like people to see my eyes. :-)

Wallace the Whale will never get you wet. The water coming out of his blowhole is silky ribbon.

make it

PREP ALL THE PARTS

1. Use the patterns on pages 117 and 118 to cut 2 whale body pieces and a whale belly. Don't forget to transfer the dots (page 87).

2. Add the eyes to the body pieces.

SEW THE SIDES TOGETHER

1. Position the ribbons at the spout marking. Pin them in place. ● ●

2. Layer the body pieces, right sides together, sandwiching the ribbons between the 2 layers. Pin in place. ● ●

3. Sew the body pieces together using ¼" seam allowance. Sew from dot to dot around the top of the body. Don't forget to backstitch.

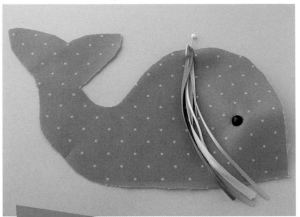

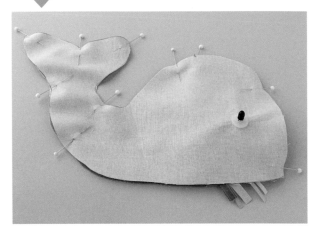

Wallace says ...

A lot of curves and points have to be matched on me! The order you pin can help you keep everything lined up. First pin the dots at the back of my belly, and then the corners at my mouth. Next pin the V in my tail fluke, and then the tips of my fluke. (My fluke is the wide part—or the fins—at the end of my tail. Isn't it nice?) Finally pin in the bend of my tail (front and back) and a couple of times around the top of my body. The trick is always to start with the easy-to-match places (dots, points, notches, corners) and then fill in around the more general curves.

ADD THE BELLY

1. Position the belly piece so that the front marking is lined up with the seam at the front of the whale and the back dot is lined up with the dots on the whale body. Pin in place, leaving a 3″–4″ opening for stuffing.

2. Sew the belly to the body, sewing from dot to dot. Leave the stuffing opening! I recommend sewing with the belly down. It'll be easier to keep the body of the whale out of the stitching if you keep it up top where you can see it.

Oops!

Sometimes, no matter how carefully you cut and sew, something just doesn't line up. I always flip my work over and check the back to make sure that my stitching went where it needed to. Sometimes this is what I'll see:

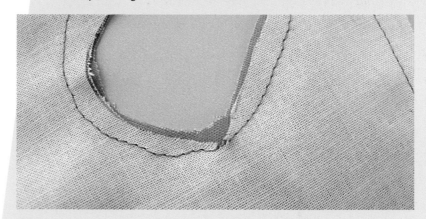

One side of the whale tail is cut a little too deep. Even though I used a perfect ¼″ seam allowance from the front, you can see from the back that it didn't quite cover the dip. If I turn this right side out and stuff it, I'll have a little hole in the seam.

Not to worry! This is totally fixable.

Sew a new section with the problem side up, so you can see it. Back up past the problem area. Line up your needle with the existing stitching and backstitch a few stitches. Now stitch forward. Instead of lining up the edge of your presser foot with the edge of the larger piece of fabric (which is now on the bottom), line it up with the edge of the shorter piece; that's the piece now on top. Stitch a new line ¼″ from that edge (it's okay to have two rows of stitching). Then gradually merge with your original seam. Backstitch to secure and take it out of the machine. All better!

FINISH HIM UP

1. Clip the concave curves around the tail, and clip once right into the notch at the top of the tail. ● ●

2. Turn the whale right side out. Work a chopstick along all the curves and points to make sure they're smooth. Press the stuffing opening smooth.

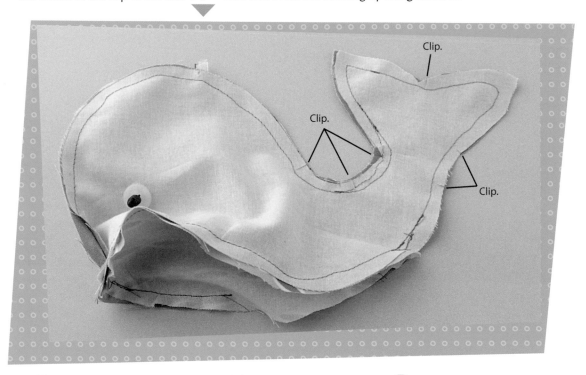

3. Stuff the flukes of the whale's tail very tightly. Use small bits of stuffing and pack them in from the tips to the stem of the tail. Stuff the stem of the tail tightly, too, but let it get a little looser where the base of the tail widens and joins the main body.

4. Stuff the main body loosely. You don't want any dips or hollows in the stuffing, so don't make it too loose. You want it full enough to look smooth and nice but soft enough for good squishing. It should feel like a marshmallow.

5. Finally, pour in about ¼ cup of plastic pellets. These will settle into the bottom of the whale body, giving it a pleasing weight and helping him stand up straight.

6. Sew the stuffing opening.

You're done. Thar she blows!

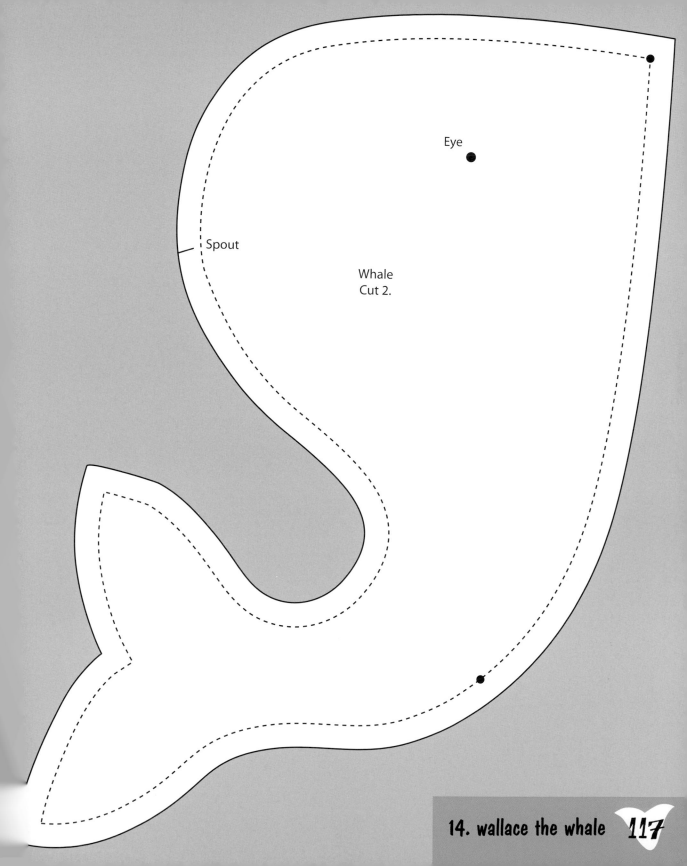

Eye

Spout

Whale
Cut 2.

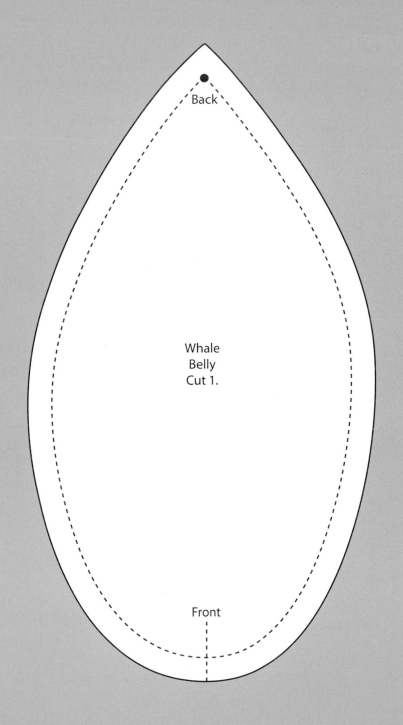

Back

Whale
Belly
Cut 1.

Front

your turn!

Caeley made a sunshine whale in warm orange and yellow. Pretty!
She used a combination of ribbon and tiny rickrack for the spout.
I love the way the wiggly rickrack looks.

Do you like the feel of the stuffing mixed with the pellets? Try it
in Henrietta the Hen (page 108).

15. sewing tricky curves

In Chapters 13 and 14, we added gussets to our softies to give them a flat base. Wallace the Whale (page 113) gave you some specific tips on how to pin those gussets in place. It's always pretty much the same: Start with the easy-to-identify spots that match up—points, notches, center points—and then divide what's left in half, and then in half again, continuing until you have enough pins to hold everything securely while you sew.

With this chapter's project, you're going to learn how to tackle two kinds of tricky matching—sewing a curved edge to a straight edge, and sewing a round base to a softie. The basic method is just the same as what you've already been doing—divide the area to be pinned into manageable (and measurable) chunks, then in half and half again as needed.

jake the jester

Finished size: 10″ tall × 3″ wide

MATERIALS

- ¼ yard main fabric or 1 fat quarter
- Scrap of fabric for head
- Scrap of felt for hat
- Fabric markers (or embroidery thread)
- Fiberfill stuffing
- Plastic pellets

Jake says …

Please choose a solid fabric for my face. It can be any crazy color you like, but if you choose a fabric with a pattern, I'll look like I have a skin disease. Or pimples!

This silly jester brings together a lot of the skills you've learned so far in a brand new shape.

make it

PREP ALL THE PARTS

1. Use the patterns on pages 125 and 126 to cut out a head, a body, and a round base. Cut the hat piece out of felt.

2. Draw (or embroider) a face in the center of the head fabric. (See Mr. Roboto on page 25 if you need a refresher on how to transfer an image.)

MAKE THE BODY

1. Sew the head to the top of the cone-shaped body piece. That's right—sew a straight edge to a curved edge. Don't worry; there's a trick. Fold the face in half and mark the midpoint with a pin. Do the same with the top of the body cone piece. Pin the center of the head piece to the center of the body piece (right sides together). • • • ▶

2. Line up the side of the head piece with the side edge of the body cone. Pin. • • • ▶

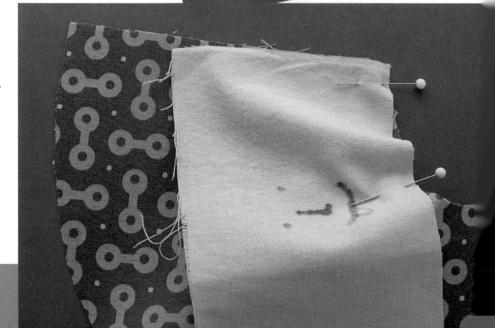

3. Add a pin between the 2 pins from Step 2. Then add 2 more pins between the center and the first pins. You've now pinned half of the curve. • • • • • • ►

It's okay if the top piece is a little ripply looking. It'll mostly smooth out when you stuff it. Plus, you'll get better with more practice. This kind of sewing is pretty advanced!

4. Repeat Steps 2 and 3 for the other half. Slowly sew the seam using ¼″ seam allowance. • • • • • ►

5. Sew the body and head up the back, leaving 3″–4″ open for stuffing. • • • • • • • • • • ►

Don't forget to backstitch at the beginning and end of your stitching.

ADD THE BASE

1. Fold the round base into fourths (in half and then in half again the other way) and mark each fold. Fold the base of the cone into fourths and mark those points with pins, too. ● ● ● ● ▼

2. Match the pins of the base to the pins of the bottom of the cone, with the right sides of the fabrics together. Pin the layers together at each matching point. Add more pins between all of these pins. ● ● ● ● ▼

3. Sew all the way around the circle.

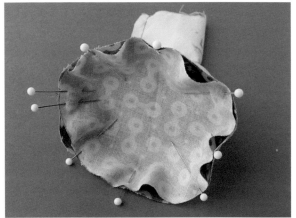

FINISH HIM UP

1. Fold the body so the top of the head is flattened, the seam is running up the back, and the face is centered on the front. Slip the felt jester hat into the opening, lining up the bottom edge of the hat with the raw edge of the fabric. Make sure the tips of the jester hat are pushed down, away from the raw edge, so they don't get stitched into the seam. ● ▶

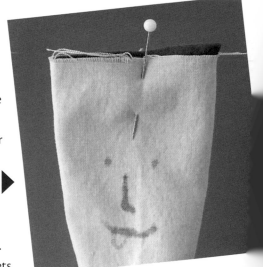

2. Turn the jester right side out. Press the stuffing opening neatly. Stuff lightly with fiberfill stuffing and pour in ½ cup of plastic pellets.

3. Sew up the stuffing opening. Done!

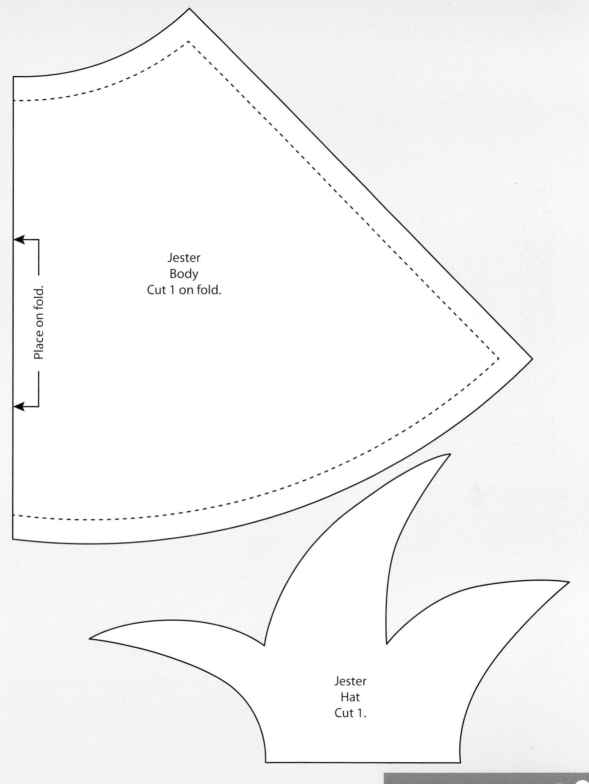

Jester
Body
Cut 1 on fold.

Place on fold.

Jester
Hat
Cut 1.

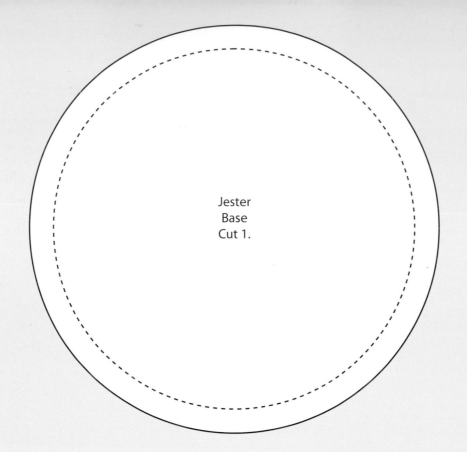

Jester
Base
Cut 1.

Jester
Face
Cut 1.

your turn!

Hana and Jo turned their jester into a king! They gave him a more serious face and replaced the jester hat with a felt crown. They even added some fat white rickrack to the bottom to make it really look like a crown. Then they glued gemstones on his crown and his robe. Fancy!

Turn it into a queen by giving it a different face and adding yarn hair or a different felt crown to the top of her head.

I think with no hair or hat at all, this would be a great flask from a mad scientist's lab! What else can you make?

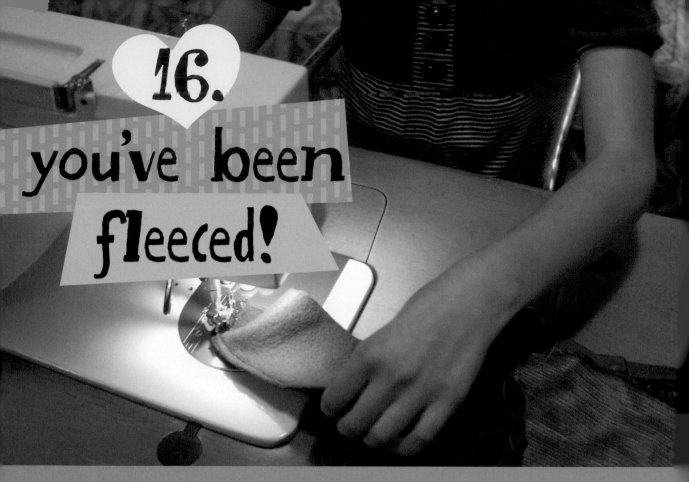

16.

you've been fleeced!

Polar fleece is delightful. It is soooooo soft and makes nice squishy softies. And it doesn't ravel at the edges, so you can sew it right side out for a different look.

Fleece is easy to work with, but it's different from the woven fabric you've used until now. Here are some tips for working with fleece.

- **Polar fleece is very fuzzy.** That makes it touchable and soft—and dang hard to mark with normal pencils or chalks. You'll get the best results with fabric markers. However, the marker won't absorb into the fabric, so it tends to sit wet on the surface for a few minutes. After you draw your lines, be sure to let the fabric sit for a few minutes before handling it.

- **If you decide to use a chalk pencil (this is especially tempting if your fleece is too dark for fabric markers to show up), be patient.** It takes a lot of back and forth for the lines to show up. Also, chalk marks tend to rub off the surface very easily, so try not to touch the fabric too much while you work.

- **Because polar fleece is a very thick fabric, you'll want to lengthen your stitch just a bit** to get a smooth stitched line. On my machine, I bump the stitch length up to 3 from 2.5.

- **Polar fleece doesn't fray around the edges,** so you don't *have* to sew it inside out like everything else we've done so far. Pay special attention to the instructions and really *think* about what you're doing. It might be the reverse of what you've gotten used to, so don't sew on autopilot.

leif the huggable tree

Finished size: 10˝ tall × 8˝ wide

MATERIALS

- 2 large scraps polar fleece for tree top (If you don't have large enough scraps, purchase ¼ yard of fleece.)

- Scraps of polar fleece for tree trunk

- Embroidery thread

- Fiberfill stuffing

Have you ever heard someone called a tree hugger? Well, this is a tree you'll really *want* to hug—even at bedtime!

make it

PREP ALL THE PARTS

1. Cut out 2 tree tops and 2 tree trunks using the patterns on pages 133 and 134.

2. Use a chalk pencil or fabric marker to transfer the face to the tree trunk.

3. Embroider the face with embroidery thread in a contrasting color. I recommend using the backstitch (page 42). ● ● ● ● ● ● ● ● ● ● ● ● ● ● ● ● ● ● ▶

PUT THE TOPS ON THE TRUNKS

1. Arrange a tree top over a tree trunk. Pin the 2 pieces together. ● ● ● ● ● ● ● ● ● ● ● ● ● ▶

2. Stitch the top to the trunk, ¼″ from the edge of the tree top. ● ● ● ●

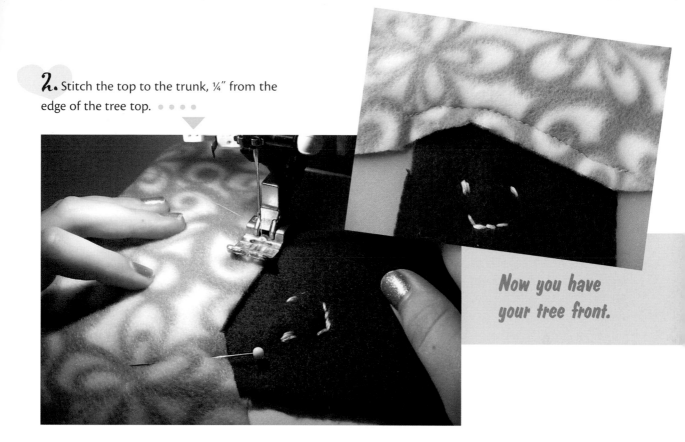

Now you have your tree front.

3. Place the tree front *face down*. Then place the back tree trunk over the front tree trunk so the edges line up exactly. Layer the second tree top over the whole thing so its edges line up exactly with the front. ● ● ● ▶

4. Pin the back trunk to the back top, making sure you're pinning through only the back pieces. Sew the back tree top to its tree trunk, just as you did for the front in Step 2.

See how the front and back pieces match exactly?

16. leif the huggable tree **131**

PUT IT ALL TOGETHER

1. Layer the front and back together with right sides facing *out*. Pin around the edges. • • • • • • • • ▶

2. Using ¼" seam allowance, sew the tree tops together around the edge. Start sewing where your stitching ended in Step 2 of Put the Tops on the Trunks. Stop sewing when you get to the start of the stitching from Step 4. Remember to backstitch at the beginning and end of your stitching.

3. If you want your thread to blend into the tree trunk, change the color in your machine to match it. Sew down each side of the trunk, from the tree top down to the bottom of the trunk. Don't forget to backstitch! • • • • • • ▶

4. Stuff the tree through the opening at the bottom of the trunk. Make sure to start with a bit of stuffing in each curve of the tree top. Then fill the large center of the tree top before working your way down the trunk.

5. Pin the opening at the base of the trunk closed. Sew it closed using ¼" seam allowance. There is no hand sewing on this project!

6. Give your little tree a hug.

Leif the Huggable Tree
Tree Top
Cut 2.

Leif the Huggable Tree
Tree Trunk
Cut 2.

your turn!

SeAnna made a tree that turns from fall to summer: one side of the top is orange, and the other side is green. Flip it over to change the seasons!

What will you do? Try making a tree for every season. Or embroider a little bird in your tree. Remember the embroidery that you learned in Chapter 5 (page 40)? Use those skills to make a bird. Or put a squirrel or cherries in your tree top. Or make a mushroom with embroidered spots. Or add an owl in a hole in the trunk! If you can draw it, you can embroider it!

Jo turned the tree into a mushroom! The trunk is the same. She just drew a new pattern for the top.

17.
fur-tastic!

Fur fabric is so irresistible and comes in so many varieties. Long fur, short fur, curly fur, colorful fur—what fun! Luckily, fur is not too difficult to work with. It just requires a little extra attention.

cutting fur

See how she's cutting with just the tips of the scissors?

If you go whacking into fur the same as you do for any other fabric, you're going to wind up with bits of fur everywhere. And I mean *everywhere*! It will go flying through the air, getting in your mouth and eyes, and settling all over the carpet. You'll be finding bits of fur months later. Your family will not be happy with you. :-)

You need to cut fur in a special way. It's not hard, but it's a slow process. You're going to have to concentrate.

You can only cut one layer of fur at a time. Flip over your fur and trace your pattern piece onto the back. Then cut out the piece, doing your best to cut *only through the backing*, not through the pile of fur itself.

When you're done, you should have pattern pieces with full-length fur right up to the cut edges—and not too many fur bits on the table and the floor.

pinning and sewing fur

You're going to take extra care here, too. Again, it's not hard; you just have to work slowly. You want to make sure that all that lovely fur ends up on the *outside* of your softie where you can enjoy it, not trapped on the inside, forever hidden. So when you pin the layers together, smooth the fur away from the cut edges first. Ideally, you don't want to see any fur sticking out of your pinned seam.

Use plenty of pins. Some furs (especially the nicest super-soft ones) tend to slip around a bit while you sew. Extra pins keep that in check.

Wrong. See all that fur sticking up?

Right. All the fur is neatly smoothed down between the layers.

finishing

You'll whipstitch the opening closed, just like any other softie. A lot of fuzz will tend to get trapped under your stitches, but don't worry about that while you sew. After you're all done and your thread is knotted off, you can go back with your needle and fluff some of the fur back out of the stitching if you need to.

Ready?
Let's make a furry monster!

balthazar

Finished size: 6½˝ × 7½˝ (not counting those fabulous long arms and legs)

MATERIALS

- ¼ yard furry fabric
- Scraps of patterned fabric for arms and legs
- 2 safety eyes, 10mm
- Scraps of felt
- Plastic pellets
- Funnel
- Fiberfill stuffing

> I love this silky, curly fur. It makes such a huggable little guy!

make it

PREP ALL THE PARTS

1. Using the patterns on page 140, cut out 2 body pieces and 4 arm/leg pieces.

2. Fold an arm or leg in half the long way, right sides in. Sew it across a short side and down the long side, backstitching at the beginning and end of your stitching. Repeat for the other 3 arms/legs.

3. Turn the arms/legs right side out (page 65). Fill each with a tablespoon of plastic pellets. That should fill them a bit more than halfway.

4. Mark the placement of the eyes on the back of one of the body pieces.

5. Back each eye with a small circle of felt that won't get lost in the fur. Use a bigger circle for long fur or a smaller one for short fur.

6. Insert the safety eyes (or sew on button eyes, if you prefer). ● ● ●

PUT IT ALL TOGETHER

1. Place the face right side up. Position the arms and legs around the sides and bottom. Pin them in place.

2. Place the body back so it is face down over the front, sandwiching the arms and legs between the 2 layers. Pin the pieces together all the way around, leaving a few inches open above an arm for stuffing. Be sure to smooth the fur down into the body as you pin (page 137). ● ● ● ● ●

3. Sew the body pieces together, using ¼" seam allowance. Flip it over to make sure you didn't run off the fabric on the back. The fur sometimes hides the edge of the fabric, so this is easy to do. Touch up any spots if needed (see page 115). Turn the monster right side out.

4. Add ½ cup of plastic pellets. Then stuff the rest of the monster very lightly with fiberfill.

5. Whipstitch the opening closed.

Be sure to smooth the fur down into the body as you pin.

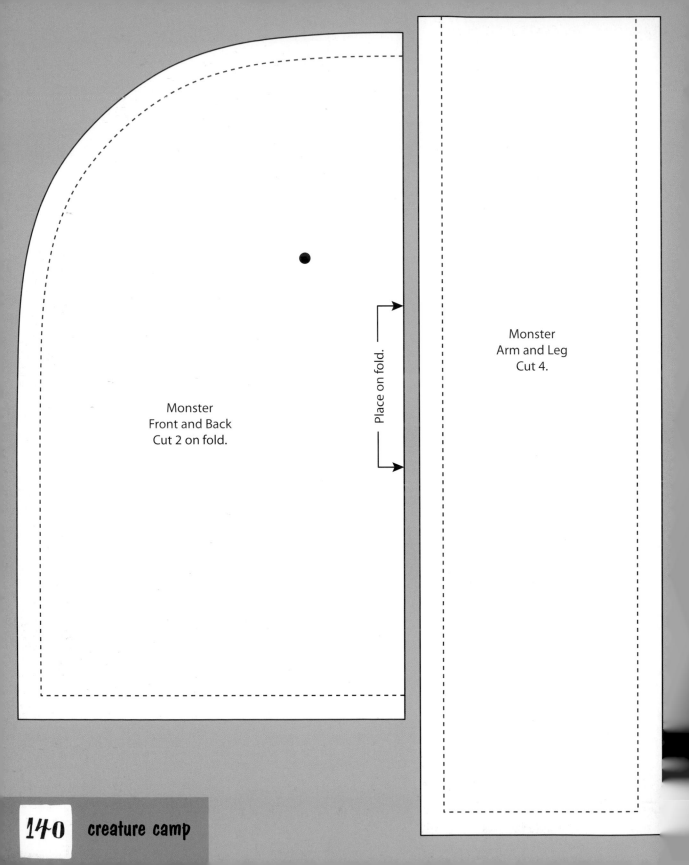

Monster
Front and Back
Cut 2 on fold.

Place on fold.

Monster
Arm and Leg
Cut 4.

your turn!

Izzy made a fabulous nonfurry monster from regular fabric. This monster does have a fluffy pouf coming out of the top of its head. That's a piece cut off a feather boa and sewn into the top seam. Doesn't it look great? I also love the way Izzy added a felt circle behind just one eye. Fun!

Jo used fur to make the monster ball on page 93.

Now, go back to your favorite pattern and make it again using fur! Hmm … a furry chicken? Or whale? You're the designer! It's OK to be a little different or completely weird! Try it! It could be awesome!

18. make it reversible!

Did you know you can make a softie that turns into something else? You can! Basically, you sew two versions, slip one inside the other, and then sew them together. No stuffing needed! The arms, legs, wings, or whatever of one softie become the stuffing for the other. Make this butterfly and see how it works.

belle the caterpillar/butterfly

Finished size: 10″ wide × 8″ tall

MATERIALS

- ¼ yard fabric or 1 fat quarter for wings

- Scraps of batting for wings

- Scraps of fabric for caterpillar and butterfly bodies

make it

PREP ALL THE PARTS

Using the patterns on pages 148–150, cut out the following pieces. Transfer the dots on both the butterfly and the caterpillar body pieces:

- 4 wings from fabric

- 2 wings from batting

- 4 butterfly body pieces

- 2 caterpillar body pieces

A butterfly *and* a caterpillar—one transformable toy that *you* can make.

MAKE THE BUTTERFLY WINGS

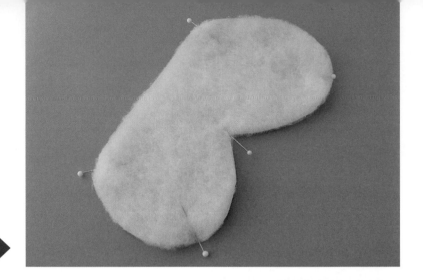

1. Place a wing piece face up on a flat surface. Place a second wing piece face down over the first. Then place a batting piece over both fabric pieces. Pin the 3 layers together. Sew all the way around the curved edge. Leave the straight edge open for turning. Don't forget to backstitch!

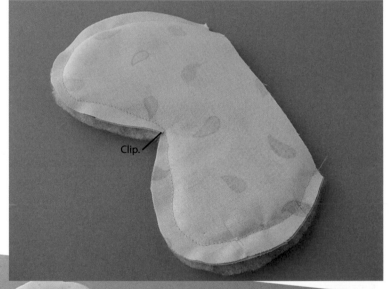

Clip.

2. Clip a notch into the sharp point where the 2 wing curves come together.

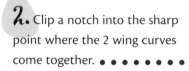

3. Repeat Steps 1 and 2 for the second wing. Turn both wings right side out. Iron them flat if you think they need it. It will depend on your fabric and the thickness of your batting.

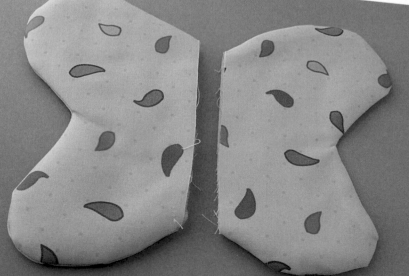

SEW UP THE BUTTERFLY

1. Place a butterfly body piece face up on a flat surface. Center a wing on the long, straight side (not the side with curves at the end). Place another butterfly body piece face down over the first, sandwiching the wing between the 2 layers. Pin the layers together. • • • •

2. Sew the long, straight edge, backstitching at the beginning and end. When you open it up, you'll have one side of your butterfly body. • • • •

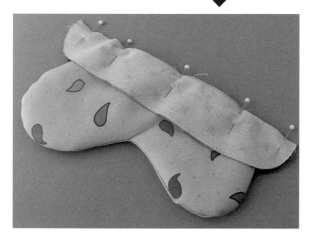

3. Repeat Steps 1 and 2 for the second side of the butterfly.

4. Now for the trickiest part. Pin the butterfly body pieces together, right sides facing each other. Flip the wings over to one side, so they come out of the body between the 2 dots on the side. Fold up the wings so they fit between the dots. It's going to be very messy looking. • • • ▶

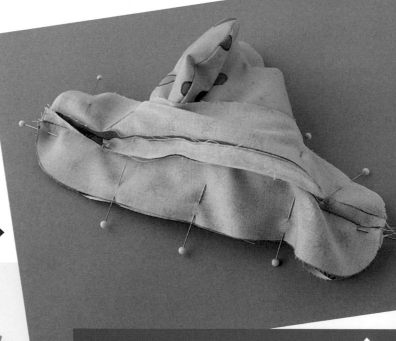

It's a mess right now. Don't worry. It's going to be a beautiful butterfly.

5. Sew all the way around the body, leaving the space between the 2 dots open for turning. Remember, it doesn't matter how much you need to squish up the wings. Do whatever you need to do to keep them out of your stitching. Backstitch at each dot! When you turn the body right side out, you'll have a butterfly! ● ● ● ● ● ● ● ● ●▶

6. Flip your butterfly open. Neatly press the raw edges of the opening. ● ● ● ● ● ● ● ●▶

At this point, you could stuff this butterfly body and sew up the opening to get a finished softie. But we take it one step further and stuff it with a caterpillar. This part's easy.

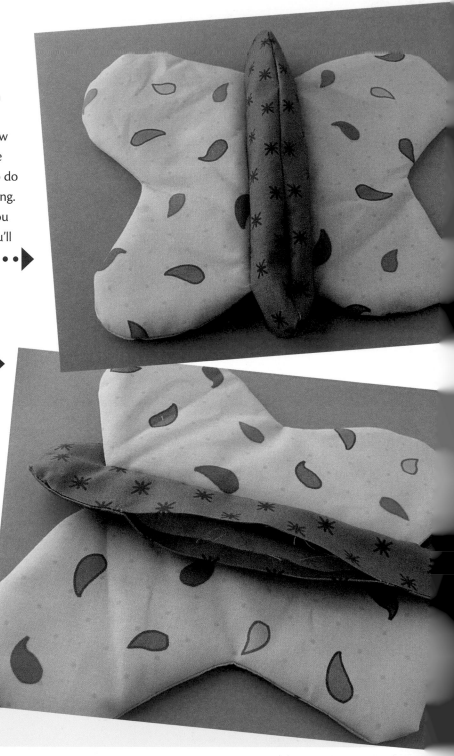

At this point, you could stuff this butterfly body and sew up the opening to get a finished softie.

SEW UP THE CATERPILLAR

1. Put the 2 caterpillar pieces right sides together. Stitch the long way around the body, leaving the space between the dots open for turning.

2. Snip the seam allowance into the 2 V's at the top of the body.

3. Turn it right side out. Neatly press the edges of the opening.

PUT IT ALL TOGETHER

1. Turn the caterpillar inside out again and slip it inside the butterfly's body. Line up those edges that you pressed so nicely. Pin them together. ● ● ● ● ●▶

2. Whipstitch the 2 bodies together. ● ● ● ● ● ● ● ●

Done! You have a butterfly!

If you turn the body the other way and tuck the wings inside, you have a caterpillar.

Jo was pretty insistent that you can't actually see butterfly eyes, but she drew eyes and a smile on the caterpillar after it was sewn up. You can do that too with a fabric marker. If you want to sew on button eyes or embroider eyes, add them to the butterfly after Step 6 of Sew Up the Butterfly. Add them to the caterpillar before you sew the sides together (Step 1 of Sew Up the Caterpillar). Don't use safety eyes. The shanks have no stuffing to sink into, so they won't look right, and they'll make the sides of your softie's body poke out.

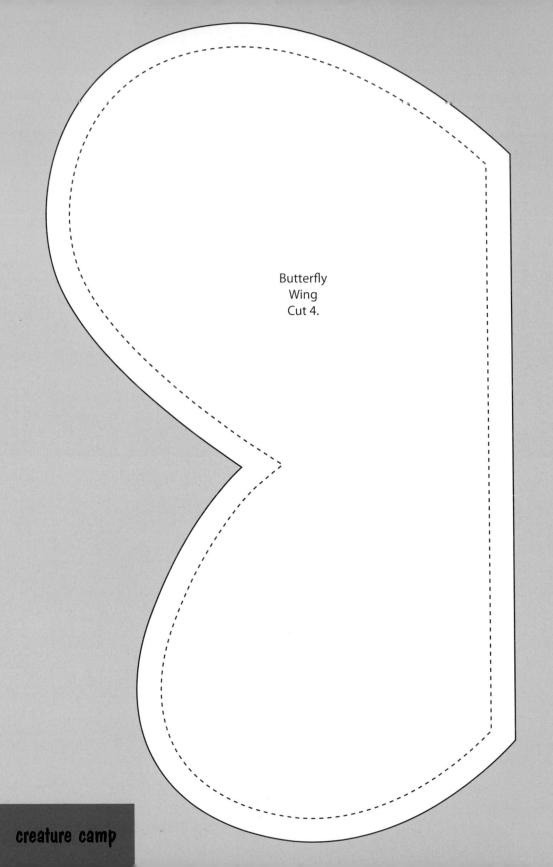

Butterfly
Wing
Cut 4.

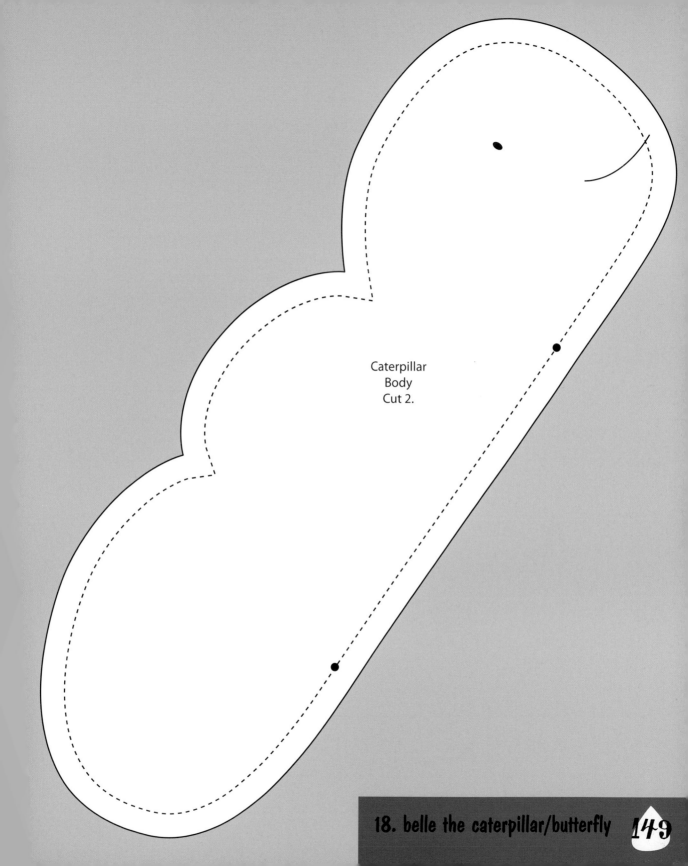

Caterpillar
Body
Cut 2.

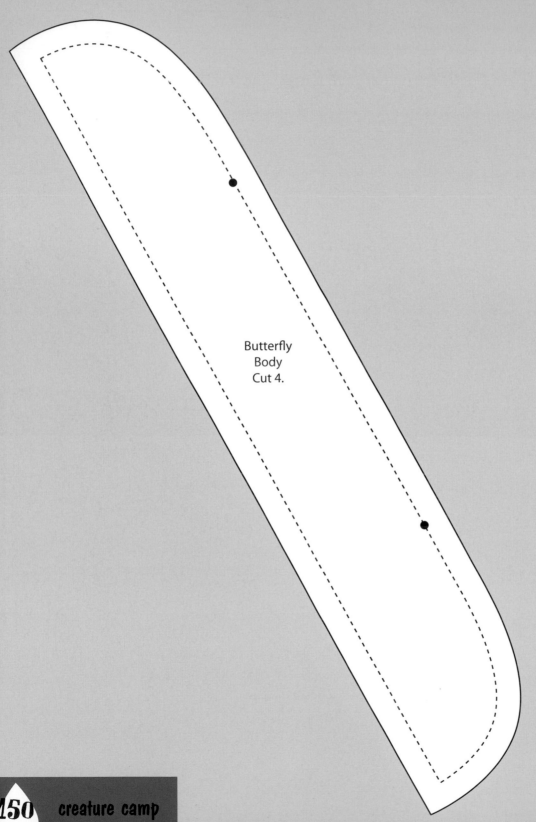

Butterfly
Body
Cut 4.

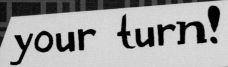
your turn!

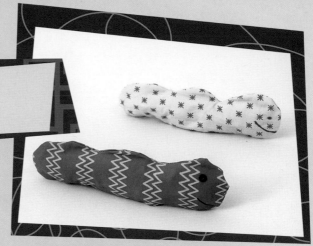

Josie drew her own designs on
her butterfly wings with a fabric
marker before sewing the wings
together. Use freezer paper (see
how on page 26) to make it easy.

19. zip it

Words to Know

LINING: Used to finish the inside of a project or to provide decorative effect. A lining is cut from the same pattern pieces as the project but usually from a different fabric. Lining in garments is made of "slippery" fabric to make getting dressed easier.

ZIPPER FOOT: A special presser foot with a narrower base that allows the seam to be closer to the zipper teeth. It can move to either side of the needle so you can sew along both sides of the zipper.

PRESSER FOOT: You've been using one all along to hold down the fabric as you sew—probably the regular presser foot for straight stitching. There are specialty presser feet for different purposes, such as creating buttonholes. Fancy!

Lots of folks are afraid of zippers (I was too before I actually tried putting one in). They're really not all that tricky. The zipper teeth in the middle look alarming, but the tapes on each side are just fabric. Zippers can be sewn to other fabrics easy as pie. Here are a few things to keep in mind:

- **Don't sew over the teeth.** They can break your needle.

- **If your machine has a zipper foot, you'll be able to sew right next to the teeth.** This tool is handy, but it's not necessary. If you just use your regular presser foot, you'll still be able to sew fabric to the zipper tape. A little more zipper tape showing on your finished piece is all that you'll end up with. Not a problem.

- **Depending on the size of the zipper pull, it might get in the way as you sew.** But that's easy to fix—just zip or unzip as needed to move it out of your way. The easiest way to do this is to sew until you're getting close to the pull. Then turn the handwheel so the needle is down in the fabric. Raise the presser foot to get it out of your way. Zip or unzip as needed. Lower the presser foot and keep on sewing.

Ready to give it a try?

zeke

Finished size: 10˝ tall × 7˝ at widest point

MATERIALS

- ¼ yard fabric or 1 fat quarter for body
- Scraps of fabric for feet and mouth lining
- 7˝ zipper
- Buttons, safety eyes, fabric markers, or embroidery thread for eyes
- Fabric markers or embroidery thread for nose
- Yarn, rickrack, or other materials for hair (*optional*)
- Fiberfill stuffing
- Plastic pellets

This project isn't especially hard, but there are a lot of steps. You have to pay special attention to whether pieces are right side up or upside down when you layer them. The instructions will tell you, so read carefully.

make it

PREP ALL THE PARTS

1. Use the patterns on pages 157 and 158. From the main fabric, cut out 1 face and 1 lower face piece. From the fabric for the mouth lining, cut 2 lower face pieces. Cut 4 feet. You might notice you're missing a back piece. No worries. We'll cut that later.

2. Make the feet. Sew 2 foot pieces right sides together. Leave the top open for turning and stuffing. Snip into the corner where the foot joins the leg. Snip right up to, but not into, the line of stitching. • • ▶

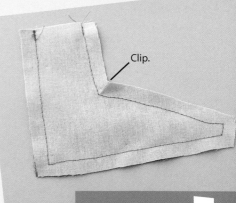

Clip.

3. Turn the feet right side out. Stuff the feet and about halfway up the legs with fiberfill.

4. Decorate the face. Jo used safety eyes and embroidered the nose. You can use buttons, markers, or embroidery for the eyes (The Eyes Have It, page 30) and markers or embroidery for the nose. You can also draw your own eyes and nose! ● ● ● ● ● ● ● ● ● ● ● ● ▶

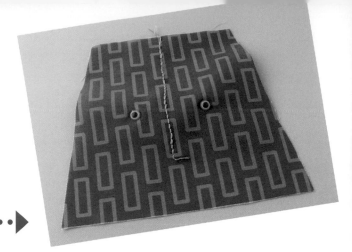

ATTACH THE ZIPPER

1. Hold the zipper sideways and take a look at it. There are teeth running across the middle, and there is tape at the top and bottom. We're going to sandwich each tape edge between 2 layers of fabric—a front piece and a mouth lining piece. We'll start with the top of the face.

2. Place a mouth lining piece *face up* on a flat surface. Place the zipper *face up* on that lining piece, so that the zipper tape is lined up with the raw edge of the fabric. Place the face top so it is *face down* over the zipper and lining. The zipper should be sandwiched between the face and the lining. Pin all 3 layers together so their edges are neatly lined up. ● ● ● ●
▼

3. Sew the edges. If you have a zipper foot, you can sew right next to the teeth. If you don't have a zipper foot, use a regular ¼" seam allowance. When the bump of the zipper pull tries to push you off your path, stop sewing. With the needle down, raise the presser foot and unzip until the pull is out of your way. Then lower the presser foot and continue sewing. This part will feel tricky until you've done it a few times. Just take your time.

When you're done, it should look like this. ● ● ● ●
▼

Double-check to make sure the zipper pull is face up. If it's face down, it will end up inside your softie. You'll never be able to zip and unzip its mouth. You'll be sad. :-(

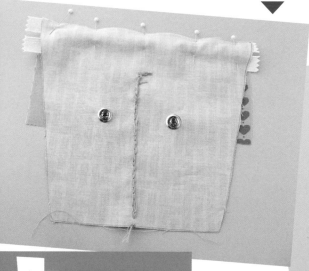

4. Now we'll do the other side of the zipper. Flip the face top and the first lining out of your way so you can work on the other side of the zipper.

5. Repeat Step 2, this time using the lower face for the top of the sandwich. ● ● ● ●
▼

6. Sew the seam just like you did in Step 3. Remember to move the zipper pull out of the way if you need to. When you open it up, it should look like this. ● ● ● ●
▼

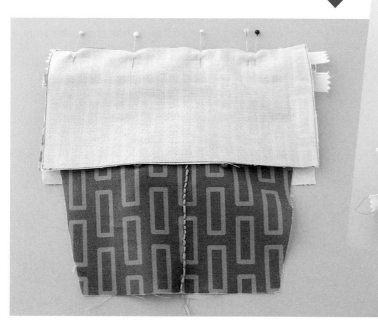

Woohoo! A zipper!

FINISH THE POUCH

Now it's time to sew up the bottom edge of that inside pouch.

Flip the face over so you can see the lining pieces. Line up the lower edges of the mouth lining pieces with right sides together. Sew using ¼" seam allowance. Don't worry about the sides. You'll sew them in with the sides of the softie.

● ● ● ● ● ● ● ● ● ● ▶

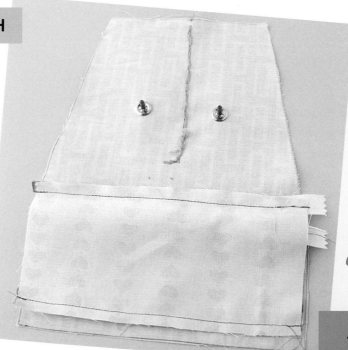

Don't worry about the sides. You'll sew them in with the sides of the softie.

PUT IT ALL TOGETHER

Now you're ready to sew the front to the back—except you don't have a back! The total height of your front piece depends on the width of your zipper and zipper tape and what kind of presser foot you used. You'll be tracing the back from your finished front— just as you did with the alligator (page 74).

1. Place your main fabric face down on a flat surface. Place the sewn front so it is face up on the fabric. Smooth everything down. Trace all the way around.

2. Cut out the piece. Now you have a back that exactly lines up with your finished front.

3. If you're going to give your guy hair, position it now. It can be really tricky to pin yarn between 2 layers. Jo just sewed hers to the face instead of trying to pin it. • • • • ▼

4. Pin the feet in place on the front of your guy. • • • • ▼

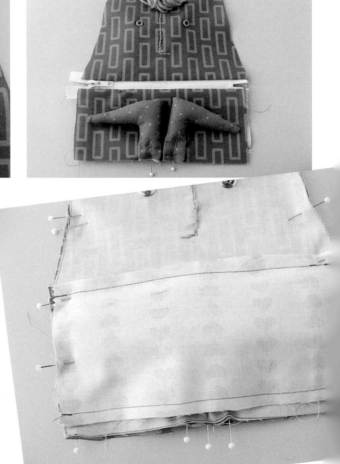

5. Layer the back piece face down over the front, sandwiching the feet and hair between the 2 layers. Make sure the mouth lining is smoothed down toward the bottom of the softie. Pin the mouth lining sides to the softie sides. The bottom of the pouch will be shorter than the softie bottom, but the sides will line up. (You will sew the pouch and softie sides in one step.) Pin the zipper tape ends in place so they don't flip over as you sew. • • • • • • • • • • • ▶

6. Sew up the body. Leave a few inches open for turning and stuffing. The top of one side of the head is a good place to do this.

7. Turn your softie right side out. Careful—the zipper can be pretty stiff. Poke out the corners with a chopstick. Press the stuffing opening neatly.

8. Pour in ¾ cup of plastic pellets. Then loosely stuff the rest of the body with fiberfill. You don't want it stuffed so tightly that you can't put anything in the zippered pouch!

9. Sew up the opening and admire! You can store all kinds of fun things in his mouth. Or you can even put an extra little gift inside.

Lower Face
Cut 1 from face fabric.
Cut 2 from pocket lining.

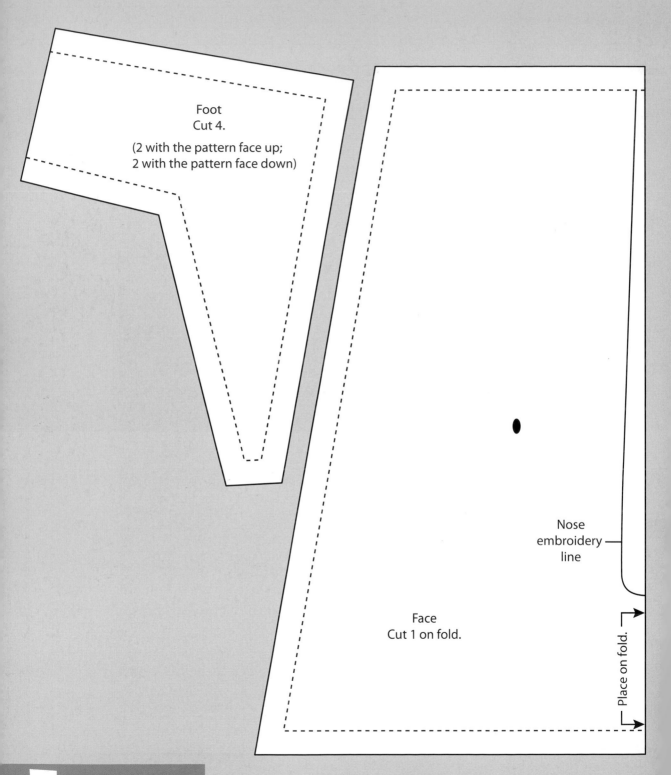

Foot
Cut 4.

(2 with the pattern face up;
2 with the pattern face down)

Nose
embroidery
line

Face
Cut 1 on fold.

Place on fold.

Hana created her own zipped-up monster. She decided against the feet that came with the pattern and replaced them with the feet and arms from Clyde the Curvy Monster (page 64). She also gave him rickrack hair instead of the yarn. She got rid of his nose altogether. Isn't he handsome?

What will you do? Add some silly arms or great big ears. You can even make him out of fur. But be sure to do that on a day when you're feeling especially patient. You can sew zippers to fur, depending on the kind of fur, but it can take a lot of fussing. Have fun creating your own zipped lip character.

20.
design your own

Throughout the book, I've given you ideas to change the patterns to make them your own. This time I'm going to show you how to make a design from scratch. If you can draw it, you can make it!

You don't need much—just pencil and paper and a ruler. A hem gauge (page 11) is the best ruler you can use, so grab that if you have one.

The other things you need are time and imagination. Designing a pattern means coming up with a picture in your head of what you want your finished softie to look like. Then you have to take it apart in your head to see how it all goes together. Here are some things to think about:

- **How big do you want your softie to be?** Small enough to fit on a shelf? In a pocket? Big enough for good huggability?

- **What kind of fabric do you want to use?** If you want fur, stick to simpler shapes. You know now that fur can be kind of hairy to work with. :-)

- **Is it for a baby?** Make sure to plan for baby-safe eyes.

- **How do you want the finished softie to feel?** Firm? Squishy? Beanie? Heavy? Light? Think about what you'll want to use for stuffing.

Because this is your first time designing, I recommend you start with something simple. Think about all the softies you've made that are basically a front and a back—Mr. Roboto, the Spooky Crew, Silly Bean People, Clyde, Balthazar. These are just a front, a back, and maybe arms or legs. They are the easiest to design.

Something like Gus the Grinning Gator is still simple, but it has extra steps, so it requires a little more planning.

For now, I recommend skipping anything that needs a gusset (like Wallace the Whale and Henrietta the Hen). You know how to sew them, but drawing the pattern for that gusset and making it fit the other pattern pieces can be tricky.

Ready? Here are the basic steps in drawing your pattern.

1. Draw the basic body shape. Make it the size you want your finished softie to be.

2. Add a ¼" seam allowance all around your softie. Set your hem gauge to ¼". Place the gauge on your pattern paper so the arrow is on the line of your drawing. Make a mark ¼" from your line. Mark dots ¼" away from your original line all the way around the piece. Connect the dots and you have your pattern piece. ● ● ●
▼

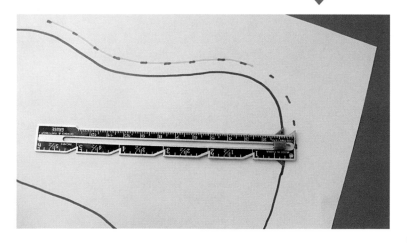

Wendi says ...

Necks are a pain in the neck. :-)

If at all possible, try not to draw anything with a neck—or any other skinny bit leading to a bigger bit. They're the Number 1 problem spot in any softie. They often flop. Sometimes they're so skinny, you can't get the head through it when you're turning the softie right side out. Even if you manage to get the head through the neck, after you stuff it, it can still be a wobbly mess. Just don't do it! Almost any animal can be redrawn to be a bit more blobby. Avoid that pain in the neck.

3. Draw any arms or legs you want your softie to have. Add a seam allowance to the outside.

4. Decorate the front and back of your softie. Add eyes and other facial features, such as freckles or a beauty mark. You need to do this *before* you sew anything together.

5. Sew and stuff appendages.

6. Place the front of the softie face up on a flat surface.

Wendi says ...

- If you want long skinny legs filled with pellets, make sure to design the tubes big enough to fit your funnel.

- Don't make arms, legs, wings, or other appendages bigger than your softie body. It will be hard to keep them out of the seam allowance as you sew.

7. Pin the arms, legs, tentacles, hair, etc., in place. Make sure to flip them to the inside of your softie. Pin them so the raw edges of the appendages line up with the raw edges of your softie.

8. Place the softie back so it is face down over the softie front, sandwiching all the appendages between the layers. Pin in place. Make sure you leave an opening for stuffing.

9. Sew the layers together. Don't forget to backstitch!

10. Turn it all right side out. Stuff. Sew up the opening. Done!

anything you can imagine!

Jo's Creation

Now I'm going to take you step by step through a real example of a softie designed and made by Jo.

Jo wanted a perfectly round softie with long, skinny arms and legs filled with pellets. Easy! She also wanted a pouch in the front to hold baby softies. The baby softies are easy, but the pouch is on the tricky side. Here's what she did.

1. She traced a cookie tin lid to get a perfect circle the size she wanted. Using a hem gauge, she added dots ¼" all around the outside. ● ● ● ●

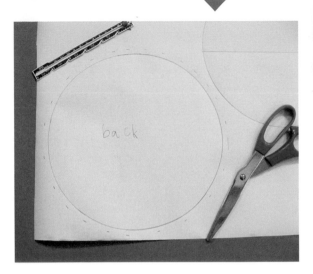

2. She connected the dots, and then cut out the pattern piece. ● ● ● ●

3. She traced the cookie tin lid again to get another circle exactly the same size. Then she used a ruler to draw a straight line across the top of the pouch. ● ●

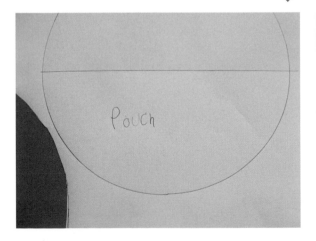

4. She used the hem gauge again to add ¼" seam allowance around the pouch piece. Then she cut out that pattern piece. ● ● ● ●

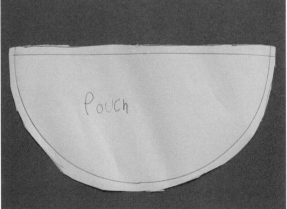

5. She liked the arms and legs on Balthazar, the furry monster, so she reused those pattern pieces. (This was very smart!)

6. She cut out all the fabric. She cut a softie front and a softie back. She remembered that Zeke had another fabric on the inside of his pocket. Even though she's not using a zipper, she decided to add a lining so it would be pretty, and also so the top of the pouch wouldn't be a raw edge. She cut a pouch piece and a pouch lining piece. Finally, she cut 4 arm/leg pieces.

7. She added eyes to her softie front. She thought she wanted to use felt behind the safety eyes, but then she spotted some metal washers that were just the right size and used them instead. Get creative with stuff you see around the house! But ask first. :-)

8. She sewed the legs and added pellets to them.

Get creative with stuff you see around the house! But ask first. :-)

9. She pinned the pouch piece to the pouch lining along the top edge, with right sides together. • • • ▼

After she sewed them, she flipped the pieces right side out so they looked like this. • • • • ▼

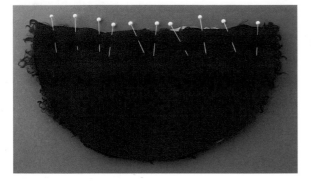

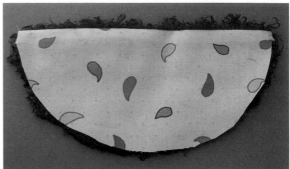

10. She was finally ready to put everything together! She placed the softie front face up on the table. She placed the pouch piece face up on the softie front, so that the bottom curve of the pouch was lined up with the bottom curve of the front. Then she pinned the layers together. The pouch and the front together will act like one front piece— just like the zipper mouth and pouch on Zeke. She pinned the arms and legs in place. • • • • • • • • • ▶

11. She sewed the softie together around the edge. She turned it right side out and stuffed it with a combination of pellets and loose stuffing. Then she whipstitched the opening closed.

12. To make the babies for the pouch, she traced a tin can and added ¼" all the way around. Then she cut the fronts and backs out of fleece, using pinking shears to give them a zigzag edge. She gave each baby a single safety eye and a little bit of rickrack hair. She sewed them *right sides out* so she could see the zigzag. Then she stuffed them with some plastic pellets and finished sewing them closed on the machine.

What will you make?

resources

FABRIC

If you see a softie in this book with stripes, polka dots, or any other pattern, I designed the fabric especially for it! That means if you want to make something with the exact same fabric we used in the book, you can! It's available online at Spoonflower.com. Search for the Creature Camp collection. It's all there! If you want to come up with your own fabric and color combinations, shop at your favorite fabric store. Remember to stick to the quilting section for the fabrics that will be easiest to work with.

STUFFING

I really like the stuffing from Fairfield. It's available from all the big craft stores. For the fiberfill, I use Fairfield Soft Touch Poly-fil Supreme. For the pellets, I use Fairfield Poly Pellets.

SAFETY EYES

I can find only black eyes at the craft stores near me. But the colorful ones are so much fun! I shop online. My favorite place to get them is on Etsy from 6060 (etsy.com/shop/6060). They sell packs of assorted eyes, so you get lots of colors in one pack. I love them!

about the authors

Photo by Wes Stitt

ABOUT WENDI

(by Jo)

Wendi Gratz has been teaching kids to sew for as long as I can remember. She sews all the time—even when she's not designing a pattern or writing a book. She's taught me and my friends to sew softies, clothes, and quilts.

Nobody taught her how to sew, but she always had the tools and materials she needed to experiment and play. She says she made some really bad stuffed animals with very wobbly necks when she was seven or eight years old, but she's gotten better since then. She grew up in lots of different places—mostly Florida and New York. By the time she graduated from high school, she had been to 18 different schools!

Making patterns is her job. She says that making a pattern isn't really hard, but it takes a lot of time. You have to be okay with making mistakes. She makes a bunch of versions (she calls them prototypes) of each new design before she's finally happy with it. She made a *lot* of versions of every project in this book before she handed the patterns over to me to make them. That's piles and piles of softies!

She carries a notebook with her wherever she goes and jots down ideas in there. She gets ideas from everything—a picture on a notecard, a dog on a leash, patterns in carpets and floors—and they all get scribbled in the notebook.

She is fun and funny and a good teacher and designer. She is also my MOM!!!!!!!!

ABOUT JO

(by Wendi)

Jo Gratz got her first sewing machine when she was four years old, and she's been sewing toys and clothes for herself and her dolls ever since. She even made a full-sized quilt for her bed!

Every year she competes in a costume contest at Dragon*Con, a *huge* science fiction and fantasy convention. She spends a lot of time every summer sewing her costume for the competition. She's won her category twice!

Besides sewing and embroidery, Jo is really good at origami, crochet, and making things out of clay. Her favorite part of making softies is stuffing them. She says it's so satisfying to watch them get fat—it's like feeding them. I loved working on this book with her because Jo is my favorite (and only) daughter. :-)